SEX EDUCATION
AND THE SCHOOLS

SEX EDUCATION

Edited by Virginia Hilu / *Harper & Row,*

AND THE SCHOOLS

Publishers, 18 17 *New York, Evanston, and London*

FIRST EDITION

Library of Congress Catalog Card Number: 67-13718
Designed by The Etheredges
I-R

CONTENTS

PANEL MEMBERS

MARY STEICHEN CALDERONE, M.D., M.P.H., is Executive Director of the Sex Information and Education Council of the United States (SIECUS), a voluntary health agency established in 1964. She is a fellow of the American Public Health Association, and is a member of the American Medical Association's Committee on Human Reproduction, and of the Family Life Commission of the National Council of Churches. She has written and edited numerous medical and lay publications on aspects of sex and contraception. She is married to Dr. Frank Calderone, formerly an official of the World Health Organization. The Calderones have three daughters and two grandsons. She is a Quaker.

MILLICENT MCINTOSH was born in Baltimore in 1898 (Millicent Carey) and educated at Bryn Mawr School and Bryn Mawr College, receiving her Ph.D. from Johns Hopkins (1926). She has been Girls Work Secretary, YWCA (1920–21); teacher of English, Rosemary Hall (1922–23); teacher in the English Department of Bryn Mawr College (1926–30); Freshman Dean and Acting Dean Bryn Mawr College (1928–30); Headmistress, Brearley School (1930–47); Dean, Barnard College (1947–52), President (1952–62), now President Emeritus.

She was married in 1932 to Dr. Rustin McIntosh, Professor of Pediatrics at Columbia College of Physicians and Surgeons and Director of Babies Hospital, now emeritus. At present she is serving on various boards: of two independent schools; Bryn Mawr College; Bank Street College; Berkshire Community College; C.B.S.; New York Public Library; Manhattanville Community Centers; United Negro College Fund, Lenox, Massachusetts, branch; Recording for the Blind. Mrs. McIntosh is one of the founders and a trustee of Kirkland College, a women's coordinate college which expects to open in 1968 at Hamilton College, Clinton, New York.

The McIntoshes have four sons, one daughter, and six grandsons.

DR. ALAN F. GUTTMACHER was born in Baltimore in 1898. He attended public schools in Baltimore until the Park School began in 1912, when he transferred to it with his twin brother, Manfred. Both graduated with A.B.'s and M.D.'s from the Johns Hopkins University. Dr. Guttmacher taught anatomy for two years, doing basic research in the physiology of reproduction. He then took a four-year residency in obstetrics and gynecology. In 1929 he joined the faculty of Johns Hopkins, rising to the rank of Associate Professor of Obstetrics, while he carried on an active private practice. In 1952 he was called to the Mount Sinai Hospital in New York as Chief of Obstetrics and Gynecology. While there he was a clinical professor at Columbia University and lecturer at the Harvard School of Public Health. In 1962 he left medical practice and became President of the Planned Parenthood Federation of America, Inc., a post he now occupies. Dr. Guttmacher has written many popular scientific books concerning conception, pregnancy, birth, and contraception. Three of his books are in paperback—one has sold three quarters of a million copies. He has also written nonpopular medical books and articles. Dr. Guttmacher has lectured in colleges and medical schools across the nation.

The REVEREND RICHARD P. UNSWORTH was educated in the public schools of Trenton, New Jersey, and subsequently at the Mount Hermon School and Princeton University. After two years as a teacher of Bible and English at Mount Hermon School, he trained for the ministry at the Yale Divinity School and did further graduate work at the Divinity School of Harvard University. In the years since 1950 he has been in the ministry to students at Yale University, Smith College, and Dartmouth College. At the latter two places he has also served as a professor of religion. He is an ordained minister of the United Presbyterian Church. His wife, Joy Merritt Unsworth, holds a master's degree in education and child development, and has taught on the faculties of the Day School (New Haven, Connecticut) and Smith College. The Unsworths have a son and three daughters.

FOREWORD

Should the school play a role in sex education? Or should this be left entirely to the family, the minister, and the physician? If the school should participate, who should teach the courses and lead discussions among the students? What should be the content of the courses? How extensive is the school's responsibility to its students to see that they are adequately informed before they go into the relatively unregulated life of a college campus? Are parents willing to entrust the school with this responsibility, or might they descend with criticism upon the school that undertakes it?

These and similar questions occupied a group of teachers and heads of some fifty schools during a two-day meeting on sex education held in April, 1966, at Princeton, New Jersey. The meeting, sponsored by the Committee on Educational Practices of the National Association of Independent Schools, was called in response to requests from a number of schools that NAIS give its member schools some guidance in this relatively undeveloped area of instruction. These requests reflected a growing concern on the part of many school heads that the time had come to overcome inhibitions and to examine realistically an aspect of education which for too long had been avoided as a hot potato.

In the course of the two days, the group was led by four distinguished discussion leaders to an understanding of the personal and cultural restraints that for several generations had prevented most adults from coming to grips with the subject. They came to realize that as educators, and as parents too, they had failed to provide children not only with essential knowledge about sex as a natural body function, but also with an understanding of sex as a basic and vital life force.

At the conclusion of the meetings, the participants were in full agreement that the schools definitely had a responsibility for sex education, and it was their strong recommendation that the

National Association consider taking steps to raise the question of sex education with its entire membership.

Acting on this recommendation, the NAIS Board of Directors voted in June, 1966, to undertake a program designed to encourage, and then to assist, its member schools with the development of programs of instruction in sex education. Mr. John Chandler, Jr., a former headmaster, was retained as a consultant, and, aided by an initial grant from the New World Foundation, the program was planned in the course of the summer and launched in the early fall with the assistance of a second and larger grant from the same foundation.

A Summary Report of the Institute at Princeton was mailed to the schools in September as a first step in bringing the question of sex education to their attention. This report was followed by several mailings designed to bring to the schools suggestions for planning and introducing a program, references to reading materials, films, and other teaching aids, and descriptions of programs already under way in independent and public schools. We were pleased to find that there were already a number of well-established programs in both. A variety of other activities have been undertaken to meet specific requests for assistance from schools, including a series of workshops for some two hundred teachers during the summer of 1967 at the University of Maryland.

This Foreword is written just about a year after the date of the Institute at Princeton. It is clear that in these twelve months much has happened as a result of it. A substantial number of the member schools of the association have initiated sex education programs of one kind or another, many others will start such programs in the coming year, hundreds of school heads and teachers have been preparing themselves to participate in these programs, parent groups have become involved, interschool discussion and communication has been stimulated, and the active interest of a sizable segment of the public has been attracted as a result of mention by the press, educational journals, and television.

We had not intended originally to publish the full proceedings of the Institute at Princeton, other than to make a rough transcript available to the member schools of the association. It was, after all, an exploratory and unstructured discussion of a complex and sensitive subject and one in which many more questions were raised than were answered. We had doubts that such a discussion, despite its extraordinary value to those who had participated in it, would be able to retain any substantial degree of its value for those who simply read about it. But the response to the *Summary Report* and the widespread inquiries received as a result of early press stories combined to encourage us to make the transcript available to a wider audience. There is little doubt that the discussion at Princeton made a real contribution to the advancement of sex education. We hope that the account of those discussions will do the same.

CARY POTTER
President, National Association
of Independent Schools

INTRODUCTION

By Fred M. Hechinger

About the only point of widespread agreement concerning sex education is that it is highly controversial. Why? Mainly because the adult community is confused not only about sex itself but also—and even more so—about the attitudes it wants to engender toward sex in young people.

As with all controversial issues, adults tend to expect the schools either to keep hands off entirely or to indoctrinate, not teach, young people in such a way that the adults' prejudices are protected and reinforced. Thus, for example, conservatives insist that the teaching of any but the conservative approach to economics is subversion, and some extreme economic radicals demand, by the same token, that youth be steeped in radical economic theory. Agreement between the opposing camps is hard to come by, and so the schools tend to play it safe and teach as little real economics as possible.

Since the views on sex are even more fragmented and the disagreements even more violent than those on economics, the schools' head-in-the-sand attitude has been even more evasive. Moreover, among those who have demanded sex education are those who have openly defied many of the conventions by insisting that what is involved is simply the teaching of "techniques," devoid of any understanding of humane, moral, and emotional questions. And at the other extreme of the spectrum have been those who tend to regard sex as something merely dangerous, to be included in the curriculum in much the same vein as the current teaching about the dangers of tobacco, alcohol, and narcotics.

Such misguided views tend to poison the atmosphere against any attempt to deal with a basic question of human growth, development, and concern in an educational manner that is at

xiii

once realistic and deeply esthetic. And yet there can be little doubt that an understanding of sex, both in the clinical sense and as a fundamental ingredient of the human condition, is part of what is so generally referred to as a boy's or a girl's liberal education—an understanding of self and others, an appreciation of the many human forces that shape the emotions of persons, families, and communities.

The need for sex education, though always real, has become infinitely greater as both the intellectual and social maturing of young people has become accelerated in modern society. The matter is not helped by the glaring and virtually unavoidable exploitation and commercialization of "glamorous" or "lurid" sex by the mass media. To let the schools evade their responsibility is to deliver young people in the most callous fashion to the worst impact of misinformation. To plead that the schools cannot hope to compete with those admittedly persuasive and pervasive influences amounts to a kind of defeatism unworthy of education. To fear that sex education will become synonymous with greater sexual permissiveness is to misunderstand the fundamental purpose of the entire enterprise.

As with all education, the teaching about sex cannot and should not be resolved through any effort to set down an all-purpose curriculum. The approach will vary as much from school to school and from teacher to teacher as does the approach to other subjects. Yet, there can be areas of agreement as to certain methods and materials as well as to the timing of such instruction. The opinions of experts and the examples of sound procedures will be invaluable in this process.

If good answers are to be found, it is imperative to know some of the pertinent questions. During the Princeton discussions among experts both on sex education and on private school administration and teaching, some of these questions were asked, without inhibitions and without an eye to publicity. It is difficult to believe that there is an educator or a parent anywhere in the country who has not asked, or heard, many of the same questions before. And so, this discussion—the asking and at least tentative answering of these questions—is truly the starting point for any sound and intelligent beginning to a program in sex education.

The very fact that the background of the experts ranged from physician to clergyman shows the scope required for any approach that may hope to lead to a successful sex education program. For what is at stake is not mere gratification of human desires nor the prevention of unwanted pregnancies nor the protection of human health, though all of these concerns are naturally part of the scheme of things. The ultimate goal, to whose attainment sex education must make a crucial contribution, is (like that of all sound and comprehensive teaching) the achievement of a better life—more humane and more fulfilling, more considerate of, and responsive to, others and more satisfying to individual and society alike. The purpose is not, as some opponents to sex education have charged, to incite—or even to aid and abet—a sexual revolution, but rather to come to a better understanding of biology and morality, of physiology and emotions, of reality and romanticism.

One must hope that not too much will be made of the fact that this effort is being sponsored by the independent schools. In many ways it is easier for these institutions, which need not ask for approval from a majority of a public constituency, to take action on sensitive issues. But once the matter has been put before the public, the lessons which are offered ought to be considered applicable to public and independent schools in equal measure. As experience, based on this volume, is gained, the benefits will accrue to all American education, regardless of sponsorship, and to American youths who stand to gain much from knowledge and free discussion as substitutes for past ignorance and fear.

SEX EDUCATION
AND THE SCHOOLS

OPENING SESSION

1. MARY S. CALDERONE

We live in an age when sex symbols are presented to us everywhere. Segments of the communications industry seem to be vying with each other to see how far they can go in presenting aspects of sexual matters at one time considered immoral. Sex images and fantasies hammer at us daily from billboards, posters, "girlie" magazines, ads for feminine products and cosmetics, comic books, movies, popular records, and books.

It hardly matters whether we salute this trend as a long-needed break from Puritan attitudes, or whether we deplore it as a shameful exploitation of relationships that should be meaningful beyond mere sensation. The fact is, it is here, and we must deal with it.

Adults, it may be hoped, can cope with this outpouring of

erotica. However, soaring rates among teen-agers of illegitimacy, venereal disease, and early unhappy marriages doomed to divorce indicate that adolescents may be lacking the standards that would allow them to form mature sexual attitudes in our era of "pop sex," or at least learn how to manage their sexual impulses.

The youngsters, I think, are doubly deceived. First, the erotic unrealities that confront them daily lend a false "Arabian Nights" aura to sex. Second, the aura of over-eroticism breeds dissatisfaction with the normal development of healthy sexual relationships that would be satisfying if young people had not been misled by fantasies. Yet, in the absence of intelligent guidelines to healthy attitudes, how can we expect youngsters to develop them? Sex instruction in the home is usually a hit-and-miss affair, with emphasis on the miss. All too often embarrassed parents mumble platitudes to embarrassed children, while most church and educational groups shy away from discussing any but the simplest aspects of sex with young people.

In schools, "sex" education is too often limited to textbook presentations of the biology of conception and reproduction. Where school programs go beyond that, they seldom stray past matters of "hygiene" (whatever that may be) for boys and girls. While this "hard facts" presentation was once a healthy antidote to earlier "birds and bees" approaches, it still offers no images of responsible, satisfying sexual relationships or how to achieve them. Without such images, youngsters have no resources with which to balance the erotic and erotogenic fantasyland that surrounds them.

Can this social lag be closed? Can children be given a realistic understanding of what sex is all about? I believe they can, if society will not only provide the basic facts its young people need, but will also create an atmosphere in which such facts can be presented effectively. As the late, great Pope John XXIII said about his Church, it is time we opened the window and let in the fresh air. Our approach should be simple and truthful, affirming that sexuality exists in all humans, and that it develops as a continuing force from birth to death. We should teach our children that this force can and must be integrated into the total personality of the individual, and that people must learn to manage it and

use it creatively and constructively in relationships with one another as men and women.

In order to begin an approach to this area of sex attitudes, sex
behavior, and sex education, six professionals in the family helping fields formed a new voluntary health organization, the Sex
Information and Education Council of the United States—
SIECUS—the organization for which I work. SIECUS does not
advocate taking the awe and mystery out of sex. Far from it. No
one wants our sexual attitudes to become casual to the point of
being pedestrian. But, by the same token, SIECUS does not advocate either of the competing attitudes now purveyed to youth
—that sexual relationships must be either an orgy or a sacrament.
Life cannot be lived solely on either of these planes. What
SIECUS does seek, in the words of one of its founders and its first
president, Wallace Fulton, is "to establish sexuality as a health
entity, and to dignify it by openness of approach, which means, in
part, promoting the concept that sex education in the best sense
involves teaching people to make intelligent and well-informed
choices among an array of alternatives."

This meeting was called by the Educational Practices Committee of the National Association of Independent Schools. That is
the right committee to consider this crucial and central issue and
to make recommendations to your member schools about the possible ways of introducing a program of sex education and of
handling it with dignity, candor, and intelligence. The real question is: if the schools are going to confront this issue, what are
they going to do? What will the practices be, in systematic, formal
sex education? SIECUS is advocating total community-wide sex
education programs. But your specific field covers educational
practices within a pedagogical situation in a private school below
college level. SIECUS has received numerous requests from public
and parochial school systems for guidelines to help them work
out programs. It should be emphasized, however, that at present
nobody has the perfect answer, syllabus, program, or pattern; nor
is there any single answer to the vital question of who shall teach
about sex and what qualifications that person or persons should
have.

We adults have allowed a situation to arise in which young

persons are constantly asking such questions as: Do you think sex life is necessary for a happy marriage? Can a mother educate her young son in ways that a father cannot? How can a girl tell the difference between real love and just sex drive in a boy? How can a young unmarried couple tell their parents they are in trouble? What shall I do when a girl friend is a homosexual and I have to associate with her at times? Why is it that when people hear that some girl is pregnant everyone thinks she is rotten and the boy wasn't so bad? Whom should I turn to if my parents won't tell me about sex? Is there any place to get some books on the real meaning of love? How, specifically, can one refuse to engage in sexual relations and still manage to show the boy that good morals won't undermine his masculinity?

The essential problem seems to arise out of a single basic fact that few people, whether parents or professionals, ever care to acknowledge: the normal, predictable, and absolutely valid sexuality of adolescence. This is new not so much to human experience as to human acceptance, and it is a fact of life that every adult who has anything at all to do with a young person will have to think about, digest, and eventually accept.

Let us talk about adolescents for a moment. What is new is the defenselessness of the adolescent today, a state for which we adults are entirely responsible. It is we who have allowed all of the protective barriers that shielded us in our youth to go down. We have done away with chaperones, supervision, rules, close family relations, and privacy from the intrusion of the communications media. We have provided mobility and luxury. As a result we have left our children totally vulnerable to the onslaughts of commercial exploitation of sex, tabloid reporting of sexual occurrences, wholly unsupervised after-school occupations, easy access to cars, and many other dangers. We have not filled the void left by the vanished safeguards with a bulwark of factual knowledge and orientation to strengthen and guide the young person in his very defenselessness about sex.

Most people will repeat their concern about the premarital pregnancies, the forced marriages, the early divorces, the abortions, the increased venereal disease rate, and the homosexuality now visibly more prevalent. I share this concern, but only because these are the disquietingly observable results of something that bothers me even more: the way in which young people ape the adults of their world in kicking around, exploiting, and treating with profound lack of understanding and respect something so valuable and central to the well-being of each and every one of them as his sexuality.

In using the term "sexuality," I want to point out that the way we use it in SIECUS has to do not with gender roles, and not with the act of coitus alone, but with the totality of what it is to be a man and what it is to be a woman in this world today. I assure you this is not easy to define. All the images we have learned are changing, particularly so as we re-examine our total relationships—racial, religious, international, interpersonal. The positive slant that SIECUS is trying to achieve is to conceive of sexuality as having to do with the quality of being sexual. A part of this, of course, is the genital or erotic. Unfortunately, that aspect has had most of our attention so far. But in the context of understanding the SIECUS use of this word we need to remember the World Health Organization's definition of health as "a state of complete physical, mental, and social *well-being*, and not just the absence of disease infirmity."

You are here as certain kinds of professionals. I am here as another kind of professional, as a physician. But, even more importantly, I am here in my specialty of public health, which orients me toward dealing curatively and preventively with the health of masses or groups of people. I am not a one-to-one person the way most of you are. I wouldn't be good at it for I am too impatient. But I can and do conceive of programs, of how one deals with groups, and of how one funnels ideas to people-in-the-mass. This is *my* specialty.

There are no authorities—believe me—in this field. It is ironic that the best people to give advice on how to give sound, adequate reproductive and sex education to children ten years old and younger are probably those who have just left that stage themselves. Any group of junior high school students would be pleased to meet with trustworthy adults and could explain in clear-cut fashion the things they themselves would like to have been taught when they were younger. Senior high school students show the same balanced perspective about the junior high school years they have just left, and college students about their senior high school years. We do not often enough accord our young people the responsible place in society that they are fully capable of and deserve to fill.

If the schools are to undertake an open and honest effort to develop patterns to fit the needs of our young, they must have the support of the parents. Physicians, clergymen, social scientists, and accredited counselors should be called in as resource people, and as the youngsters reach adolescence they also should be involved in consultation and planning.

I have already mentioned that there are no authorities in this field. We in SIECUS have published three discussion guides: *Sex Education, Homosexuality,* and *Masturbation.* Now stop and think: masturbation, not premarital sex, is probably the key area of difficulty because, although it is a universal phenomenon of every age, it is impossible for almost any adult to consider it with equanimity. Yet SIECUS was able to get consensus to publish from our board, a group including two Catholic priests, a rabbi, a protestant minister, physicians, social scientists, and several representatives of the Kinsey group. From this wide spectrum, we managed to produce a pamphlet that opens the door to discussion. *Yet we are not authorities.* The masturbation pamphlet that we publish today might have to be altered radically two years— or two months—from now. Yet we would not have been capable of writing such a pamphlet a year ago, this we know. I simply tell you this to indicate that the climate has changed and that society seems more willing to contemplate and consider man and the many and varied aspects of his sexuality.

The schools are not alone in their concern, and you must remember this always. I want to emphasize this over and over again. Numerous others are seeking navigational aids. For several years, as a member of the Family Life Commission of the National Council of Churches of Christ in the U.S.A., I have been aware of what some church denominations are doing. Several SIECUS members are meeting during the summer for a week or ten days at a time with counseling groups of the major church denominations.

You will have the support of physicians in your community. Already in several of the major professional publications there have been papers on sex education. Medical schools are conducting all-day symposia. The Colorado Medical School sponsored a symposium on sex problems in medical practice that drew the largest attendance of any single medical meeting in the history of the state.

The young people are with you. I spoke to fifteen thousand teen-agers, Future Homemakers of America, in Oklahoma City, broken up into three sittings—Friday evening, Saturday morning, and Saturday afternoon. On the morning after the first sitting, fifty of the teen-agers from that session and I had a question-and-answer period. After the two and a half hours, the court stenographer who was recording the session said to me, "This was an eye opener. I am most profoundly grateful. I am not married, but I can tell you that I see the other side of sex in my courtroom. I will never forget this morning and those young people; I want to thank you deeply for what you have helped me to understand."

So think of yourselves in context now: do not feel lonely, for *you are not alone.* You are part of an enormous mass of people in this country who have in a short space of time been reached with a positive message: that sex is not a problem to be controlled. It is instead a creative force that we must learn to use and to manage in all of our relationships. People are not nonsexual and never will be—they will not be nonsexual when they get to be seventy! We are never neuters, even on the day we are born.

As we sit here we are talking about our toddlers, our children, our adolescents, and our young men and young women. Nothing we adults can do to help these young carry successfully the burden of "freedom with responsibility" should be too difficult or too painful for us to undertake. Their need is great, and if sometimes the way seems hard for us who are in the middle years, let the words of one of my young questioners echo in their poignancy: "Even though there are no clear-cut morals and virtues, do you think we as Americans could define our own so that we will be the type of citizens the world needs today? This age and pace make it awfully hard to do, for there are so very many demands."

2. MILLICENT McINTOSH

I am speaking tonight from the point of view of a teacher, a headmistress, and a college executive. In addition, I have had the enlightening experience of listening to my own children and their friends, and of reading the *Harvard Crimson*. So my approach will be a direct, practical one derived largely from a somewhat diverse experience. One important element in this entire discussion has not yet been mentioned, and that is the parent. Everybody is on our side, we say. In undertaking to discuss what the schools should do in the area of sex education, however, the parents must never be overlooked. Nor can we overlook the fact that educating parents is a major problem, almost as challenging as that of educating our students.

I recently served as a consultant to a small private school. One night I talked to the faculty about the problems and the opportunities facing the independent school during the coming years. One of my points was that as independent schools we are as free as we can make ourselves be to tackle the current problems of students and of their parents. Among these problems is that of sex education. Afterward a biology teacher said: "What are we going to do about our parents? Suppose I say things to my class which imply a different sex ethic from the ethic of the parent. What happens then?" We may talk at considerable length about the responsibility of the school in this area. But every program structured for the purpose of educating children about sex and about reproduction, every school that has a program, and each school contemplating a venture into this area must always come back to these important figures—the parents. What does one do about them, about their ethical standards, about their usually strong views?

I went, as a young woman, unmarried, in 1930, to head the Brearley School in New York. It was at that time an extremely conservative school for girls, founded in 1885 to prepare for entrance at that time to Bryn Mawr, and later to all of the other women's colleges of the East. But, fortunately for me, about ten years before I came, the Brearley School had developed a new lower school. In the lower school they had animals which were cared for by the children in each of the classrooms. In the fourth grade they had an incubator, plus various parts of the reproductive system of chickens and all other kinds of animals. A pig that made his lodging there for a short time spent quite a lot of time in my own basement on Eighty-seventh Street, because we couldn't cope with him at night in the school.

So I found myself in the midst of an extraordinary framework for sex education. One of the first excitements was a group of first graders who were tenderly caring, with cotton batting, for a female rabbit who was pregnant. The moment came when the science teacher said: "We must separate the mother from the father, put the father in the closet, and leave the mother in the midst of the cotton batting." She took good care to explain to the children that the father might be jealous of the babies, and might be anxious to do away with them. The next morning the babies were born—in the closet. This long-remembered incident gave me a sense of humility about the whole idea of sex education, about whose responsibility it is, and about the wisest approaches to use in educating our boys and girls in this area.

We developed from this a course in physiology in the sixth grade. I was now married and the mother of twin boys, so I was considered a good candidate to talk to the sixth grade about what it's like to have a baby. This is something that has since become a Brearley tradition. When I meet Brearley girls now, everywhere over the world—my husband says if I would go up Mt. Everest I would find one of these Brearley girls—they say to me, "Oh, I remember sitting on your floor, and talking about having a baby."

What happened to me, of course, was that I was practically forced into this kind of "sex education" by the circumstances of living in New York in a civilization where tabloids existed, where Errol Flynn was a hero from time to time. I had great assistance from Benjamin Spock, who happened to be our Brearley doctor for fourteen years before he became famous. Of course, *we* thought he was famous at that time. I remember, with Ben Spock, trying to cope with the discovery in the sixth grade of three books which had been found among the belongings of a girl who had the German measles. Her father had been in the army during the First World War and had collected three of the most astonishing books that you have ever seen: one about a homosexual school for girls in Paris, one about sexual perversions, and one which included every imaginable kind of picture. Ben Spock and my doctor husband went white to the lips when they looked at these books.

When I left the Brearley School and went to Barnard, I appraised the situation from another angle. When you see the products of the schools coming into the colleges, you are immediately aware of one inescapable fact. These boys and girls arrive with a fully developed feeling of their own independence, their own sexuality, with little feeling that there is anything evil about this, and with a strong feeling that adults have not given them the help they needed. Where the children needed guidance, they received dictates from above. In the colleges, one is constantly told by students that in their schools open and candid discussions on sex were seldom if ever held. And those of us who have worked with young people have been told over and over again by the students of their lack of opportunity to discuss with their parents all those adolescent problems with which many of us are familiar. So the youngsters are thrown full blown into the colleges, free to do what they want. What are their guides? The attitudes of their friends, and the books they have read; the constant pouring into their consciousness of advertisements, television, and plays—the fully documented sex appeal of our society. Many of them have absorbed the point of view of parents who have not always lived the kind of lives themselves that they are willing to talk about with their children.

So one major problem, it seems to me, is not merely giving sound courses in the physiology of sex, or even arranging frank discussions of adolescent problems such as masturbation or petting. It is finding ways of *creating the right point of view,* in co-operation with our parents. The children go home at night, if they go to day school; or they go home for weekends and holidays from a boarding school. If they repeat discussions or ideas given them at school which are unsympathetic or frightening to parents, a major conflict is at once established. No matter how scientific, how wise, how liberal teachers may be, they must come to grips with the fact that parents have to fit into this picture somewhere, and the schools must work out a practical approach to their presence.

3. ALAN F. GUTTMACHER

I feel very diffident in this area, because I am not sure I qualify as an expert. As an obstetrician, when I occasionally go to court,

I am asked some stereotyped questions. First, "What faculty positions do you hold?" Second, "How many babies have you delivered?" My stock answer to the latter is, "Seven thousand." I do not know the exact number, but that is a good round figure. Then they will say, "Doctor, you have delivered seven thousand babies, but in addition you have been the director of several academic obstetric services. How many deliveries have you supervised in your long career?" So I think deeply and say: "About a hundred and four thousand." Then, of course, I qualify as an expert.

Here I have no such qualification. Therefore, I think I shall give you a few biographical notes. When I was a youngster in Baltimore, we had a strange and delightful invasion from New York in the person of a woman, Laura Garret. She was the Executive Director of the Social Hygiene Society. Apparently some parents, including my own, were sufficiently liberated to allow Miss Garret to teach us sex education. This began as "nature walks," when we were about twelve or thirteen years old. We walked coeducationally—and Miss Garret was delightful. She was a rather ample-hipped woman, stocky in build—a kind of mountaineer type—and about her was the unmistakable aura of the outdoors. On one occasion the most remarkable phenomenon happened. We were walking in an area of Baltimore called Dickyville, and Miss Garret was about two paces ahead of the group. Suddenly she halted. There, lying in the gutter on the side of the road was a dead mole. Miss Garret always carried with her her dissecting materials. She knelt down and dissected this little beast and—you won't believe it—the animal was pregnant.

This, then, was my introduction to the uterus and to the fetus. I do not know yet whether before the walk began Miss Garret planted the small creature there or whether it just appeared through the intervention of a sympathetic Providence. At least it was the most remarkable coincidence I have ever been subjected to. In any case, Miss Garret's "nature walks" began my interest in sex education. Then, too, fathering three daughters did not diminish it. Since I was in a somewhat liberal city and involved with a somewhat liberal school, the Park School, which my children attended, I talked to the headmaster, Hans Froelicher, about the possibility of teaching my children and other children something about sex. He took the bait, and we decided to initiate it at the fifth-grade level.

It was an interesting experience for me, and I think for the children. I probably approached the topic much too mechanistically for most of you. I took pregnant rats, properly killed, to dissect. I put spermatozoa under the microscope. I washed eggs from the Fallopian tubes. When I began the first class the boys sat in a little group over here, the girls sat in a little group over there. There was tittering back and forth; they all looked ill at ease. Within fifteen or twenty minutes they had all thawed out so that they were soon interspersed as far as sex was concerned and asking questions in wild excitement. The four or five classes I held each year for several years, I thought, went extremely well. A number of parents called to thank me for having done this for their child. I didn't get a single call from a parent who objected to it.

I enjoyed this experience, and missed it when I moved to New York. There I had no such connection with young people until my children entered the upper school at Birch-Wathen. At a parents' tea, I met a young man, Victor Harris, who taught science, including physiology, to the high school. I said to him, "Mr. Harris, what do you do about the physiology of reproduction?" He said, "Oh, Dr. Guttmacher, I skirt around it. I'm not very comfortable with it." So I said, "Let me do it." Well, you should have seen his face. This was great, from his point of view.

Perhaps these limited experiences qualify me as a pseudo-expert —I am not an expert—furthermore, I question whether any of us are. I think each of you is as expert about all of this as am I.

There are five things we ought to ask ourselves:

1. Shall we teach sex education and family living?
2. At what age level? Does this need to be repeated in the various grades? If so, how often? As you know, in Sweden they repeat it every year, beginning with about the age of eight, when the children are in the second grade.
3. What should be the content of such courses? I say *courses* because I think the subject should be repeated several times during the school life of the child.
4. How do you do it? What are the teaching techniques? How im-

portant are movies? How important is assigned reading? How important are laboratory demonstrations?

5. Lastly, who is going to teach?

These are difficult questions to answer. But they must be tackled so that some wise, intelligent steps may be taken in the right direction.

4. RICHARD P. UNSWORTH

I grew up in an era when, the day before we were to be married, Father or Mother sat us down and said: "Now, Son, if there is anything you need to know, be sure to ask me." My wife and I both had this experience. We were determined to do it differently. So after our first child had arrived, and the second was on the way, my wife sat Sarah down—Sarah was then about three and my wife was bulging precipitously—and started in to answer her questions. Being a zealous mother and an educated woman, she answered many more questions than Sarah asked. After Sarah had sat patiently through what got to be a fairly lengthy lecture, Joy sat back feeling fairly satisfied with the new role that she had fulfilled. As a liberated mother, she suddenly thought of something, and turned and said to Sarah, "Sweetie, why did you want to know all of that?" And Sarah said, "I didn't want to know all that. But, Mother, please open your mouth again; I just want to shout down hello to the baby!"

We have come full circle, I think, to a kind of liberation of mentality about sex and education concerning sex. We have been liberated by Freud from our Victorian cocoon. As we have been liberated, I am afraid that what has come out has been not a butterfly but a moth—a moth which is fascinated by this new light but doesn't always know when he is being illumined and when he is being burned. We are in the position—and our young friends in college, and younger, are in the position of being— very confused about sex—liberated, to be sure—open—healthy-minded in general—anxious—and uncertain—above all, I think, confused. And it is because they are confused, and because we recognize that we are partly responsible for their confusion, that a discussion like this takes place. Last night I sat at the supper table with Sarah, who is now twelve, and said, "Sarah, tomorrow I am going to be talking to people who are teachers and head-masters at schools, and who have the responsibility of educating hundreds of children. Now, you are a sixth grader. We are going to be talking about sex education. What do you think I ought to tell them?" Sarah said clearly, "Three things: (1) Make sure that they start it early enough." I interrupted her—she's in sixth grade now—and asked, "What's early enough?" She said, "Fifth grade." I asked why fifth grade, and not fourth. She said to me with great condescension, "Don't you think fourth grade is a little *young* for that sort of thing?" But her point was, start early enough. (2) Her second point was, *talk to the boys and girls to-gether*. I asked her why, knowing that in our school system they start the girls' sex education one year earlier than the boys'. She said, "It saves the girls a lot of time, because they just have to turn around and tell the boys anyway." This says something about what we think is the lack of communication between boys and girls of that age on matters of sex. (3) Her third point was that I ought to talk about the *morals* of sex, and I asked her, "Why that?" She said, "Well, we get lots of facts. I think I know all that I can know about sex, how the reproduction takes place, menstruation—all of these things—but no one in the class ever talked to us about any of the moral sides of sex. So you ought to talk about the morals of sex." I thought maybe this was just be-cause I was a minister and she's my daughter. But as I quizzed her more about this, I became convinced that this wasn't simply prejudice. She was bringing up a legitimate concern.

We need to talk about the morals of sex. Eros has come into its own in our times in a way that it has not at any time in the his-tory of Western Judeo-Christian civilization. Eros—erotic love—has lived under a cloud which Jews and Christians alike created. Under Hellenistic influence, the Christian Bible, the New Testa-ment, took an extremely acerbic attitude, on the whole, toward sex. I used to be defensive about this, and tried to say that the Bible had a healthy mind about sex. I've decided that it doesn't have a consistently healthy mind about sex, at least St. Paul didn't. My authority here is a Biblical theologian who pointed out that the context of thinking in the Bible has not provided us with the guidelines that will be useful now when Eros has come

into its own and when we can now talk freely, and with real openness and appreciation, of the positive values of sex and sexuality.
We need, therefore, to talk about the morals of sex because we
don't have many good guidelines to help us in thinking about
them.

The Christian tradition has been frankly deficient in providing
us with the sort of insights we need to deal with the liberation of
sex in our time. This is not to say that the Christian faith lacks
useful moral insights regarding sex. But the elevation of women
from a status of subordination to a status of partnership with
men has happened only in this century, and that has set the
ethics of sex in an entirely new light. Christianity's deficiencies
show up most sharply in the face of the new questions raised by
the equality and independence of women, the population explosion, the changing character of marriage and family structures,
and rapid advances in the realm of control of life (conception,
contraception, abortion, etc.).

One thing has to be guarded against. In our enthusiasm to be
liberal-minded, open and affirmative, we may overlook the fact
that sex, while not immoral, can be nevertheless used immorally.
We can be so careful, so wary about being moralistic—and liberated churchmen are now especially prone to wariness of being
moralistic—that we can overlook the real moral concern that we
must have, the real moral concern we must be able to share with
the young as part of the process of sex education. There is need
to recover a freedom to deal as directly with the morals of sex as
we have become free to deal with the facts of sex. It seems to me
that our present mood is changed, but we have not necessarily
solved all our problems. We used to fear the facts and push the
morals. We are now, I think, at the stage of pushing the facts and
being a little bit fearful of the morals.

Anti-moralistic thinking about sex is proper thinking in one
important respect: it emphasizes the fact that the healthy approach to sex education and to the moral concerns about sex
cannot dwell only or excessively on what is proscribed, forbidden.
It cannot dwell on the dark and forbidden transgressions of sex—
that is generally where we have put our emphasis when we talk
about the morals of sex. That kind of preoccupation establishes
guilt and anxiety about sex and sexual behavior, which then spill

over into other areas and lead to profound confusion about the values of sexuality and about sexual practices. Anti-moralism is a kind of antidote to the misuse and misappropriation of sex, a very important antidote.

When we remember how prudish we have been taught to be on the question of sex, how defensive we have been about pornography, we may be helped by the statement of the Catholic theologian Bernard Gilligan, who said: "You must remember that prudery and pornography are prurient brothers under the skin."* Part of our communication with the young has got to be against a backdrop which remembers that prudery and pornography are indeed prurient brothers under the skin: our own prudery, our own tendency to lapse into prudery, is really evidence of our own pornographic preoccupations more than it is evidence of a sense of decency and proportion about sexuality.

5. DISCUSSION

DR. CALDERONE: This is in no way a rebuttal—it is rather a rein-
forcement, in gratitude for having some of the things said. Incidentally, I am a Brearley graduate, and I can never forget the
day when Miss Littell slit down the abdominal skin of a frog,
laid it back—and revealed the marvels of the inner world. It
was incredible. It was so beautiful, so orderly. I think I was
thirteen.

In the public school systems I see a tremendous movement.
In many places, the powerful PTA's are encouraging the administrators, who are quite understandably cautious. As this
movement grows in the United States, it is trying to involve
all leadership elements in communities in programming, planning, and acceptance of a total community program. We at
SIECUS are saying, "You cannot go any faster in the community than the community itself is willing to go." If the
community will accept something at the fifth-grade level only,
then that is the level at which to start. From there, one can
expand up and down, all the time continuing the education

* *Cross Currents* (a quarterly journal), vol. XIV, no. 2, p. 128.

of the total community. The parents must be included in this educational program. In many places they themselves are taking the leadership since a number of them are teachers, physicians, and vitally interested in the public school.

It has frequently been said to me: "You cannot teach sex in the public schools without teaching morality. You cannot teach morality without teaching religion. You cannot teach religion in the public schools, therefore you cannot teach sex." One cannot teach *anything* in any school without teaching morality. In the social sciences, history, or English literature, how can one *not* deal directly with the moralities that underlie any and all human relationships? There is an ethic in every discipline. I would not isolate sexual morality outside of the general framework of all morality. Where it fits in each particular religious framework is, of course, up to each religious communion to handle.

Reproduction education is not to be confused with sex education. Our children know that by the time we get around to reproduction education we should be far along in sex education. Straight reproduction should be fully mastered by the time the child is ten *at the latest*. Meanwhile, the background and basis for sex education are being laid, for teaching of responsible sexuality and responsible parenthood really begins in kindergarten.

One does not decide whether or not one will have a program of sex education. Sex education is going on at every instant of a child's life. The culture impinges on the child instantly at birth, with the father's and mother's attitudes about themselves and each other as man and woman. This is sex education. It goes right in through the pores. When these attitudes are faulty, the distorted results are seen later on. So what we are really asking here is, what kind of systematic education should there be in schools specifically. How can we counteract the negative aspects of what boys and girls are already getting from their culture? We cannot choose at what levels we will have a program in sex education. We do it at *every* age level. We need to determine the formal framework to use, and what benchmarks to establish. By five, our children come to us with the attitudes we see. Therefore, at five we must start; and at seven, nine, or eleven we must have certain benchmarks. All of the children must have had a similar basic background. And it will be far better for them and for us all if they have the guidance not of their playmates on the block but of responsible, sympathetic, and perceptive adults.

MRS. MCINTOSH: I don't think we can leave the morality of sex to the church. Everything that Dr. Calderone has been saying is intensely concerned with the morality of sex. This is one point I'd like to make.

We are deeply concerned as educators with the effect of our modern sex approaches on personal and on married life. For example, when I went to Barnard in 1947, it was just before the first of the Kinsey reports came out. A little later, the report on females came out. I feel very deeply the kinds of mistakes that we made at that time, particularly those made by a person like myself who regarded these reports as being very specialized and only for psychologists, and who took seriously the criticisms of those professionals who said that these statistics were not important because they represented a selected sample, self-selected. We should have been much more alarmed by those reports. We should have gotten to work right away. We are now reaping the results of our neglect as we try to learn what happens to marriages as a result of freer sex experience.

The Kinsey report on women makes it clear that a woman who has had sex experience before marriage has a much easier and quicker response to the sex experience after marriage. But what the report is concerned with is a *physical* response. There is nothing in the index of the Kinsey report about love, children, happiness, family.

Is there any research set up to show the effect of premarital relations on the woman in marriage afterward? What kind of family does she have? What does she teach her children? Or haven't these studies been going on long enough? This is one problem that we really haven't faced up to.

The effect on the personality and on the family of the newer approaches and the newer freedom of sex is a deeply moral question that we've got to concern ourselves with before we are in any position to give opinions to the young about sex ethics. I don't know what to say to them, and I don't think that biology teacher with whom I was talking last night knew what to say. What *should* we say?

DR. GUTTMACHER: I can only echo what Mrs. McIntosh has said. I don't know what to say either. I was asked to talk to the freshman class at Barnard. I said, "You've come to the wrong person. I can't do it." They said, "Why not?" I said, "Because I can't tell these girls whether it's right or wrong to have premarital intercourse. I don't know." And they said, "We don't know either." I said, "All I can tell them is to be sexually responsible, that is, responsible to their home environment and to themselves as human beings—and, of course, to be sexually responsible not to create an unwanted, unplanned life." They said, "We think that's what these girls need to hear."

The colleges are certainly confused, as are we, the teachers.

REV. UNSWORTH: I want to mention William MacNaughton, who is now at Princeton University in the counseling department. Before that he was at Dartmouth. Mr. MacNaughton systematically studied values in college students, and he has considerable light to throw on what happens in college to values and attitudes on sex and sexual behavior. I live amidst students. To find out what they are thinking, I read MacNaughton! They tell him; they don't tell me. They come to me when the girl is pregnant and they are trying to figure out whether to marry her or not.

Another person who has much to add to our dialogue is Vernon Eagle, Executive Director of the New World Foundation.* His foundation is one of the few that is willing to risk money on important social problems where independence and daring are a necessary part of seeking creative solutions. Mr. Eagle has written, "Pathfinders cease being explorers when they are overtaken by settlers." Perhaps we can hope to discover how to keep the independent schools from being "settlers."

Let us talk candidly of independent schools and how really independent they are on the questions of sexual attitudes and behavior. Independent schools have traditionally justified their existence on the ground (among others) that they are independent of public pressures and governmentally exercised

* The NAIS program in sex education has received major support from the New World Foundation.

restraints, and are thus free to experiment and to lead the secondary school world in meeting new educational challenges. They have also said that their freedom permits them to "take a position" religiously and/or morally with regard to the values they would like to communicate to their students.

Ironically, the independent schools have played their hand cautiously on some of these matters out of fear: fear of conservative trustees, fear of alienating parents (who might deprive the schools of income or prestige by withdrawing their children), or fear of their public image in the community. Speaking frankly among ourselves, we often admit that independent schools have put a higher premium on respectability than they have on venturesomeness.

We have to learn about the role that independent schools can play in taking leadership in sex education in context. By *context* I mean the context of family life, values, and social concerns. Perhaps independent schools can make some strides here and set down some accomplishments which will be of help to the public schools.

I can imagine, for example, that some independent schools could develop a complex of curricular and extracurricular approaches to the problems of social-sexual maturity which could be tested, proven, and recommended to public schools. The latter are usually less free to be experimental, so the independent schools have both the privilege and the obligation to do some pathfinding.

The colleges are not doing much of a job in holding up standards, in dealing intelligently and openly with questions of sex education and affirmation of standards in sexual behavior. We need all the helpful advice we can get.

At Dartmouth there is an explicit statement on this matter in the handbook. As soon as you start getting explicit, the college students want to know exactly what you mean by this explicit statement, and then you are in trouble. When I was at Dartmouth we tried putting in the following phrase: "The College requires high standards of morality, good order, and gentlemanly behavior of its students both on and off the campus." In regard to the entertainment of female guests, we add: "Lewdness and fornication constitute violations of college standards." Try to be dean of a college and live with *that* one for a while! You tell me how to do it differently, or better, and I will carry that message home to the dean, who has been waiting these many years to hear how to do it differently or better.

I was thinking earlier of the forsythia and the blossoms in New Jersey. In the spring the administrator's fancy really turns to thoughts of young love and its indiscretions. College administrators are beleaguered with questions when, at spring house parties, the students mount mattresses on their heads and dates on their arms and head for the golf course in an edifying show of masculine uncertainty. We do not know the wisest response to make at all. One could simply tighten up on regulations and police every nook and cranny of the campus, looking for violations of the "gentlemanly conduct code." But the impracticalities of that approach are matched only by the indignities it heaps on student and administrator alike. Our desire, like yours in the schools, is to be open and understanding on the one hand and to provide useful models and helpful guidance on the other. Our dedication, after all, is to young people. That is one of the reasons for being an educator. And part of that dedication is our commitment to help them in their own struggle toward independent maturity, a maturity whose shape we cannot control or perhaps even forecast. Let me express my own hope that the college people among us will derive some helpful ideas from these conversations, and will see some new approaches to the problems of meeting our responsibilities to the students you yearly hand over to us.

SECOND SESSION: DR. CALDERONE

DR. CALDERONE: Before I start, I would like to ask Mr. Foster Doan, chaplain of Blair Academy, to give an account of the reactions at his school when I spoke to the students about sex.

MR. DOAN: Well, Dr. Calderone spoke to our boys. Since then, we have been deluged with letters, almost all totally favorable. We now have parents who are coming to school. They seem to feel that we have some mystical formula because at least the "word" has been mentioned for the first time. Out of several hundred letters, we have had two unfavorable ones. One said, "Why aren't the Ten Commandments good enough for us to follow today?" The other one said, "Sex is not a topic that should be discussed in a school." We did not tell the parents or the boys that Dr. Calderone was coming or what her topic would be. Since her visit, however, the discussions among the student body have continued red hot. What Dr. Calderone has done

for us has been unbelievable. Not only have we started discussions in school, but we are also now carrying on an almost-
weekly discussion with a nearby girls' school. We have been
able to add a number of good books to the library. Among
them are Clark Vincent's *Unmarried Mothers,* Kirkendall's
Pre-marital Intercourse and Interpersonal Relationships, and
Wendt's *Sex Life of the Animals.*

DR. CALDERONE: An issue of *Family Life* carried a little article by
P. Q. Houdek, a marriage counselor and the Executive Director of the Kansas City Social Health Association. In this
article, "Youth's Unasked Questions," Mr. Houdek lists the
questions asked in a survey with children. These are the
questions children say they would like to have answered in
their lives, questions they would like to ask their parents but
never dare. There are such questions as, "Why don't you
understand me?" that illustrate uncertainty about themselves,
especially in the eyes of their parents. There are other questions about parents, such as: "Why did you divorce my father?"
"Tell me about my real mother. What was she really like?"
"Why don't you become Christians?" "Father, why do you
drink so much and make us all completely miserable?" One
section is made up of questions revealing what the children
must have thought to themselves and also their concerns about
their future in family relations: "Is Aunt Genevieve going
insane?" "Can I get married when I am seventeen?" "Mom
and Dad, will you help me to be a student and to be real
popular?"

I want to read all of the questions about life: "Is marriage
nothing but responsibilities and heartbreaks?" "What is the
difference between an adult and a child?" "Do you think I
should respect someone who doesn't act in a way to get respect?" "How do you become a mother after marriage?" "Why
do girls of seventeen and eighteen get married so quickly?"
"I am having too much fun now. Why do I have to grow up?"
"Why was I even born?"

In a real sex education course, kindergarten through grade
twelve, those questions would provide good opportunities for
discussion that might lead to self-answering.

What are our immediate goals, or what are our goals for a

sex education course? Most people are glib at explaining what they want sex education to accomplish, and many will say: "To prevent illegitimacy or veneral disease." Others will say: "To prevent sexual activity in certain groups of people, preferably adolescents, college people, and poor people." There are still others who will say that they want to promote happy marriages, and they often have cookbook recipes for this. Marriage and sex manuals are seldom based on scientific study and observation, but rather on the personal biases and experiences of their authors. Manuals tend to rely on tricks and techniques, as if a relationship between a man and a woman can be covered by a cut-and-dry recipe. I call this the "cookbook approach," and I am not for it; I am also not for cookbook manuals to tell our children about sex.

We in SIECUS feel that these criteria are operating at either poor or tangentially relevant levels of motivation. If a family planning program has as its main goal to reduce the number of people, much would be accomplished. But more will be accomplished if the primary motivation is not to reduce numbers but to enhance the quality of living for every individual that you are reaching, especially within the family unit.

My two personal goals for sex education are the development of individuals with a mature and rounded sense and acceptance of their sexuality as an integral part of their total personalities, and the development of individuals capable of using their sexuality as responsibly and creatively in all of their relationships as they would any of their other endowments, physical, intellectual, or spiritual.

So, in a sense, the achievement of sexual selfhood and its use throughout the life span in creative ways are our main goals.

Any educational process depends on three factors for its effectiveness: (1) A strong body of knowledge in the area being explored and in related areas, made freely accessible to the students in an orderly fashion. (2) Opportunity for open discussion under skilled leadership, to cover not only the pure facts but also the areas that are open to question, to differences of opinion on philosophical, ethical, or religious grounds. Openness and the willingness to discuss, to answer any question no matter how distasteful, should be the emphasis. One of the questions asked of me at a men-only session at a large university was: "How does it feel to have an orgasm? What happens in the woman?" Another question was: "How do men have homosexual relationships? What is it that they do?" One should be able to answer these with candor and with dignity. An honest question deserves an honest answer. (3) Strong motivation in the students. This, I believe, we can take for granted!

Sex knowledge is not available and, if it is, it is not freely accessible. In the private schools, for the most part, the books, the talks, and the courses are not there. With *The Scarlet Letter,* for example, in most English classes everything is discussed except the central theme. Obviously, an important aspect of the book is the way adultery was looked upon in that epoch—the woman's punishment, the man's punishment. This could be a wonderful springboard for an open discussion of differing ways of looking at adultery. Today it adds luster to the image of many a film star, or so it must seem in the view of the young. Unhappily, our teachers don't dare venture into such discussions.

For the most part, parents have not opened the door for discussion of sex either, with the end result that their children have arrived in college with a host of questions unanswered, unprepared to cope with the freedom of college life. The only "guidance" that they have had is the literature that they have read outside of school, the constant pouring into their consciousness of advertisements, television, and the movies and plays that they have seen, the fully-documented sex appeal of our society.

We have a large body of knowledge about the reproductive system. We are able, more or less objectively, to make this available to our young, although always too late. In the McGraw-Hill film *Human Reproduction,* whose remake I helped with, there are numerous simple diagrams about the various male and female organs. This film was originally made for colleges to be used in conjunction with a textbook in college health. In remake, it is suitable for lower age groups because it is simple, factual, and objective. But actually it may not even be suitable for high school students. It may strike them as being too simple and boring!

We have knowledge about the reproductive system. About the sexual system as such, we are nearly illiterate. I would like to distinguish between the two systems. They share some organs in common, but the main target organs are different, as are the functions. The sexual system is used throughout mature life, at least, and certainly earlier in many cases, *as* a sexual system. But even in the female it is comparatively seldom used *reproductively,* and I can hazard the guess that a male in our society acts *sexually,* with *reproduction* a by-product.

The neural and hormonal pathways differ in the two systems. We do not have good definitions for the normal functioning of the sexual system. Whereas any medical student can define easily the normal function of any other system in the body, with the sexual system we do not have the base lines for "normal" functioning. We should always put that word "normal" in quotes. "Normal" functioning depends on who you are and where you are sitting at the time. This, of course, is far too open for a scientific interpretation.

We do not have answers to such questions as: "To what degree and of what quality is homosexual behavior an expected or perhaps essential part of sexual development?" We are getting away from using the term "homosexuality." That is a diagnosis. Homosexual behavior is an observation, and there are many forms of homosexual behavior at all ages, of some of which we may be quite unaware or even approving.

Let me come back to the difficult question of masturbation: What, if any, is its role? It is a well-nigh universal phenomenon. Is it one way by which one comes to know one's sexual self? Is it essential to the development of sexuality in the individual? Is it a way by which sexual tensions can be harmlessly released at a critical point in the life of the individual—in adolescence, after marriage, during periods of illness or separation, with the termination of marriage by divorce or death, or in such involuntary celibate situations as prison or the armed forces?

If it is not to be considered normal but pathological, how should we classify it? *Any* masturbation is dangerous, as in narcotics? *Some* masturbation is dangerous, as with cigarettes?

Too much masturbation is dangerous, as with alcohol? Or is it perhaps *the use* to which an individual puts masturbation that is dangerous? Is the person using masturbation as an escape, as a substitute, or as a compensation? These questions *must* be answered, because if masturbation is dangerous, medicine and science must devise means to control it and indoctrinate the individual to do so. Or, if our society is neutral about it, we should tolerate and ignore it, and consider it entirely the business of the individual involved. If it is useful, science must indicate in what way it is, and how to safeguard its usefulness.

Now to the question of open discussion, of the freedom of accessibility to what knowledge we have. Students are far readier than we to be comfortable in accepting knowledge and discussion about sex.

So we come to the teacher's role. I refuse to say that the teacher is the only person. I say that *all* professionals who deal in a guidance capacity with young people in any way should be involved. Every specialty is involved, and the role of the professional should primarily be one of *affirmation* regarding the validity and importance of sexuality.

From the therapeutic point of view, the high school level represents the golden opportunity for the school to make up for previous deficiencies. They are many. Children reach you in high school with many unanswered questions, no matter how open the family has been. At this point the parent-child relationships are becoming strained, so that this emotion-laden area piles an extra burden onto the relationship.

Also, from the point of view of preventive medicine, the high school age is probably the last chance to arm the individual. Once he gets into college it is too late. He will take with him his misconceptions, his incomplete information, his preconceptions, his experiences uninterpreted to himself, whatever sexual experience he has had. And by then he will really be in the rebellious age. The rebellious age has moved up into the college, and we are not going to be able to reach the student except where good counselors who have no connection with the administration are available.

Most high school students don't feel they can talk freely

to counselors who are in any way connected with the administration, so this is a golden opportunity. If you really want to find out what to teach in high school, over Christmas or Easter vacation get together a group of college freshmen who left your school the year before and ask them what you failed to do to prepare them for what they met when they got to college. You'll find out all right.

We have to bear in mind the four main tasks of adolescence as defined by Hornick, a psychiatrist: (1) Separation from parents. (2) Definition of sexual role. (3) Establishment of a value system. (4) Choice of a vocation. For those who are not going on to college, we give some help in the schools with the fourth, but practically none with the first three.

The two most critical areas are: definition of one's sexual role and establishment of a value system. In struggling with the first, the young often overthrow the second. This is a source of deep guilt for them. They see all around them adults doing exactly the same thing—men trying to prove their masculinity by knocking over one girl after another while at the same time mouthing platitudinous moralities to their own young.

Sex education must be part of a total health education program. The Bronfman School Health Education Study of the N.E.A. revealed that right across the board the main areas most glaringly deficient were, first, sex education, and second, family life education.

The Public Health Committee of the New York Academy of Medicine, in its critique of the Bronfman Study, fastened on these two glaring lacks. Of all the things that should be done to develop interest in other phases of health, this committee felt that most important should be to deal directly with these anxieties in the young about sexual selfhood. They felt that once you had satisfied these anxieties you would then be able to lead the young into awareness of needs in family life education, interpersonal relationships, and all other levels and phases of health.

I should like to see a course in reproductive biology offered in every high school, to fulfill the science requirements for those who are not going on in science. It should be designed as a bio-social approach to the facts of life itself.

It should cover the anatomy and function, the physiology and endocrinology of the reproductive and sex organs in animals and men. Ovulation, spermatogenesis, fertilization, conception, gestation, birth, contraception, infertility, and the whole process of reproduction should be taught. So should the development of the embryo—whether tadpole, chick, or human. Genetics would be important; everyone wants to know about the Rh factor, and about sex determination and what conditions are inherited. There are magnificent films on these subjects. I have seen Richard Blandau's film on ovulation and egg transport in the rat, in which you see the cluster of stained blue cells in a live anesthetized rat actually carried down the Fallopian tube. Seeing it this way means far more than a diagram on a flat page. I want our children to see such films.

Child development and nurture—a marvelous word—are of great importance. We have learned how early childhood conditions affect the individual in maturity. No one is a homosexual or a prostitute at birth; society makes us that way. The effects of emotional or physical deprivation, the absence of a father figure, broken homes, abandonment—we must learn how to avoid or compensate for these if we are to eliminate alcoholism, homosexuality, narcotics addiction, promiscuity, and delinquency. Our studies of promiscuity show that the compulsively promiscuous girl rarely experiences orgasm. We accept that narcotics addicts and alcoholics are ill people; we are beginning to understand that many such distortions have their roots in early childhood. If our teen-agers are to become responsible parents, they must be taught the effects of emotional deprivation in infants.

In this course in reproductive biology, there should be a thorough study of the family and society. Not all children take social science, so it is important to discuss the institution of marriage, its history and its endurance in some form in every society. There should be consideration of the factors that today threaten marriage and family stability.

Finally, man must be studied in relation to his environment

and to his resources; this is part of reproductive biology, the way man poisons and pollutes the environment he must have to survive. The relation of population to man's future must also be studied, and family and population planning discussed.

We often talk about the disastrous effects of early marriage. The Vincent study on *Unmarried Mothers* is an excellent one for young people to read at this time, with interpretation. Early marriages are undesirable because they so often end in divorce, and leave a child to be brought up by a child. If young people realize this, they may then perhaps have a stronger motivation toward postponement of sexual expression. We are not a postponement-minded people! Young people see their parents having what they want when they want it.

In this opening up of new ways of thinking, new attitudes, we have to help young people take many small steps in relationship to the development of their own sexual selfhood and that of others. We need to involve our young men in a feeling of responsibility for the young women whom they knock over so easily!

This kind of approach is closely involved with male-female roles and the maturation process. We isolate our teen-agers out of the main stream of life. We do not give the adolescent a significant role to play. He is a nuisance, and so we send him away to boarding schools and let the masters and mistresses look after him. If he is in the home, he is upstairs with his record player. We say, "Stay out of our way. Be off; don't bother us. Do not ask us to let you in on the serious business of running society. Particularly don't ask us to give you jobs or to involve you in, let's say, the Head Start Program, because it's too much trouble." We don't give young people the meaningful role to play for which they are not only ready but also hungry, and which would in its turn help them develop their sense of meaningfulness as people, their sense of their sexual selves as coming men, or as coming women.

That is why SIECUS is working from the point of view of involvement of a total community in a sex education project— all the churches, all the schools, all the adults in adult education, all the community agencies, and the parents.

I don't like to get up on a platform before fifteen hundred

people to speak on "Sex and Social Responsibility," then ask for questions and stagger off with four hundred written questions which I have no opportunity to answer. All I can do is to leave the questions in the community, and say: "Analyze them, tabulate them, circulate them. These are what your youngsters are asking." Almost more than anything else, this will prove to the parents how much and what needs to be done.

Now I would like to pick up some of Alan Guttmacher's five points. First, "Shall we teach?" We cannot decide whether we shall or shall not. We *are*. So the question really is, shall we teach consciously and well, instead of unconsciously, carelessly, and destructively. Yes, we must teach. Secondly, "At what age levels?" Well, this is a continuum. A five-year-old comes into kindergarten already with a great deal of sex education, much of it negative. In the so-called good sex education books, the emphasis is that the father and mother have intercourse only in order to have a baby, and that this is a passive, nonemotional act. The father "places" his seed in the mother. This, in fact, is not what happens. The sexual relationship has a tremendous emotional content; it is on-going throughout the marriage, and once in a while a particular act might result in a baby. If you tell five-year-olds that this is the way fathers and mothers reaffirm their love for each other and that science and religion have made it possible for parents to choose when they will have a baby, you are teaching responsible parenthood, responsible sexuality, right in the kindergarten. We need to get over the fear of communicating to the young that marriage brings with it this great relationship. It is a closeness that husbands and wives have all of their lives together, and they will have this experience even as grandparents. This should be made clear to the young, immediately. In a church situation this can be interpreted as part of God's plan, as the way that has been given to men and women to reaffirm the fact that they have chosen each other as husband and wife first, not as mother and father first, but, I repeat, *as husband and wife first.* The nonemotional approach should not be for the young. Instead of presenting this experience as a sort of clinical, white-tiled operating-room thing, it should be told as the emotion-laden experience which it is, totally private to man and wife—deep, powerful, communicative, and restorative—what Dr. Leon Israel calls the conciliatory role of coitus—what I call the healing grace of coitus.

"At what age levels do we teach this?" All the way up, repetitively, expandingly.

"What content, when?" Certainly by the age of ten, our children should already know about reproduction, responsible parenthood, and responsible sexuality—the facts and the attitudes. Between the ages of ten and thirteen, we need to talk about the family, responsible interpersonal relationships, marriage, illegitimacy, feelings that have to do with one as a boy or as a girl, and how to understand another person's feelings. We need to explore how differently boys and girls feel about all of these things. Let them express these differences.

For ages thirteen to fifteen: discuss the family within society, as well as the individuals within the marriage, male-female roles; illegitimacy, abortion, infertility, control of fertility, human relationships and the need to expand them. There should be something about homosexual behavior. Every boy in an urban environment is going to have a homosexual advance made to him, and therefore he should understand what it is and what his attitude about it and about himself should be, and how to handle it. This is important. I know of a boarding school boy who came back after a holiday and went to pieces for several months. It took time and counseling to find out the cause and then persuade him that he was not a homosexual because a man had made an advance to him in a public washroom.

From fifteen on up, boys and girls would thus have an excellent background for discussion of any and all social issues related to human sexual behavior. Remember, though, that many will come into the schools without any background. You are going to have to catch them up, make sure that they all get it. But from then on, as their own maturation develops and unfolds at different paces, you must keep coming together for continuing discussion, so that there is no anxiety that is not aired, nothing that is not answered.

For young adults there needs to be a continuing re-examination of sexual behavior between individuals, the techniques of courtship and dating, and the whole panorama of marriage. One of the questions I get from girls is: "How can we stop our mothers from forcing us to date so early?" This often shows a concern for the oncoming younger brothers and sisters. I think we *should* involve them in concern for the younger ones, and in open discussion of all these areas.

In talking to young people I often use the simile of driving a car. Pressing that accelerator pedal is just the greatest, but if that is all you know about driving a car, you are not a driver, you are a real danger to yourself and to everybody else. There is a lot more to learning how to drive a car. Of course, applying the brakes, obviously. But how? Under what conditions? Snow, mud, with a flat tire, rain, ice, sand, around a curve—all to be learned about applying the brakes. You must also know the rules of the road, whatever they may be, wherever you are. You have to learn to judge the other fellow's actions and reactions: his speed of approach to you, his speed of moving away from you, what you think he is going to do. You also have to know your own car pretty well: how does it corner, how top-heavy is it, where is its center of gravity, how easy is it to overbalance? You have to learn all of these things before you should depress that accelerator pedal, *if* you want to be a good, safe, productive driver. I think it is a pretty good simile, and one that has meaning for the young. It is not that we want to stop them from driving a car—not at all.

Good sex education gets away from the genital level, into other areas of questions and attitudes and relationships. This is the key, really, to lift the sights of our children to how human beings relate to other human beings, whether they be older men and older women, younger men and younger women, or each other.

DR. CALDERONE'S QUESTION PERIOD

QUESTION: *You use nothing but clinical terms. When you are dealing with children, they use the old four-letter, Anglo-Saxon terms. Do you think it's necessary in dealing with them at their level to keep it clinical?*

DR. CALDERONE: I think it's necessary to do that which is comfortable for them and comfortable for you. I did use the word "fuck" once on a public platform of a high school and the skies did not fall in. I did it deliberately when a question gave me a golden opportunity: "Why do some boys like to talk dirty in front of girls?" So I immediately twisted the thing around and said: "It depends on what you mean by talking dirty, and what the fellow means. I have actually heard the word 'fuck' used in a good and clean way. I have heard the word 'intercourse' used in a dirty way. So, it depends on the *motivation*—what you mean. . . ." Now, I didn't answer the original question, "Why do some boys like to talk dirty in front of girls?" That wasn't important to answer. But I did what I did deliberately to see what would happen, to see if anybody would be shook up. Nobody was.

COMMENT: For years now we have brought to our school every fall a psychiatrist and a medical doctor, and have gone through this discussion carefully with every faculty member. We have asked each faculty member to do exactly what you are suggesting, answer every question, go into it fully. I can assure you that *The Scarlet Letter* is being discussed wholesomely and fully, and so is every other piece of literature where the opportunity arises. A number of us are trying to something about this.

DR. CALDERONE: Of course, many public schools are quietly doing this, too. But SIECUS does not issue a list of the schools where sex education programs are in existence because we have no way of evaluating them. Sex education at one school may be just a one-time lecture on menstruation! As I emphasized earlier, sex education in its broadest sense is not a one-time event. It should be a *continuous process,* an all-pervading one.

QUESTION: *That gentleman talks in terms of having sessions with the faculty, and farming out through the individual faculty the chance to have this kind of discussion with students. That's precisely the point at which I run into difficulty. As the headmaster of a school, naturally I am omniscient, omnipresent! Maybe I am qualified to do this, but I am not sure that I can trust this whole responsibility to the faculty members. It seems to me that one of the key points is, what is the individual's own experience? Through what experience is all this filtered?*

DR. CALDERONE: I know just what you mean. You want to make sure it is done right. This is a good question, and I am convinced that in every school there are individuals who are well fitted to do this, with little more preparation than the freedom to approach it. They are mature individuals who are comfortable with their own sexuality. Now, obviously we need to identify such people. Let me give you an example. The State of Kansas has had a program going jointly with the Departments of Education and Health and the Medical School, an excellent program involving principals, superintendents and teachers, in peripatetic workshops. In a meeting at the University of Kansas Medical School, several years ago, on school sex education programs, one principal said: "In my school the Latin teacher would be the best one to handle the subject." This was a perceptive statement. You state where you are. You identify the individuals who are most ready to go. In some schools it is the coach. In other schools, it is *not* the coach. The most open discussion I have ever had on any campus was at a Catholic women's college with about six or eight nuns not just sitting in the back but joining in. The students were mature, sophisticated young women, highly educated, obviously the cream of the crop, and their questions were pointed. Their discussion was open, some of them had obviously had premarital intercourse, but there was no question that they were comfortable in discussing the relational aspects of it, with me and with the nuns. There was no problem at all in talking about some of the things that were troubling them. Marriage is not the main factor. It is the maturity of the individual.

QUESTION: *Are you saying that if you farm out the job indiscriminately it won't work?*

DR. CALDERONE: Yes, you have to start slowly. You cannot force a teacher of English to talk about adultery in *The Scarlet Letter* if he or she isn't ready to. But you can lead him to it. You can have this kind of discussion in faculty meetings, and uncover attitudes. If the students bring up as a matter of course the idea of adultery as one of the many social problems in this particular book, you have made a beginning. I use this simply as an example. Theodore Dreiser's *An American Trag-*

edy is a tremendous book to start a discussion. So is Updike's *Rabbit, Run*. The little film *Phoebe* is a good one for a school to see, with the proper preparation. The film is done in a kind of Fellini *8½* way. It is about a young girl who gets pregnant, and her fantasy of all the ways she could tell her boy friend, her mother, her father, her teacher. Then she has fantasies of all the ways it could come out. At the end, you just see her picking up the phone and in the hearing of her mother say to her boy friend, "I am going to have a baby." She slams the phone down, and that's the end. It's an open-ended picture; you never really know how it comes out. But, as a discussion starter, it is excellent to show to parents or teachers, and to use as a discussion starter in groups of young people.

QUESTION: *You accept the principle that* who *teaches is more important than* what *is taught?*

DR. CALDERONE: How it is taught is the most important of all. Also there is need for opportunities for students to sit down in an open session and discuss. The teacher lecturing is not as important as open discussion.

QUESTION: *How about the great pressure on us to get boys and girls into college and our own fear of diluting that effort with what some might consider as "side issues"?*

DR. CALDERONE: We are discussing not a side issue but a central one. To use this as a reason for not confronting this crucial area of the students' lives is to continue to do a disservice to children and to society. All the Ph.D. and M.D. degrees in the world can't create happy, sexually integrated and successful men and women.

COMMENT: I gagged on something you implied a minute ago; that *who* teaches is more important than *what* is taught.

DR. CALDERONE: You may omit some facts but the basic attitude is one of great importance.

QUESTION: *But suppose my attitude is one of complete openness, and my ignorance is one of completeness?*

DR. CALDERONE: Ignorance if acknowledged can be compensated for, but, if one's attitude is wrong, there may be trouble ahead.

COMMENT: I am not sure that children do not learn a great deal from people whose attitudes are "wrong."

DR. CALDERONE: They do learn, unfortunately.

COMMENT: I mean they learn things that are helpful.

DR. CALDERONE: Yes. This is one of the difficulties, because the children instinctively know. A perceptive comment made by a young girl was: "One of the troubles with grownups is that when they talk to us about sex, they don't want to *educate* us, they just want to *control our morals.*" How perceptive that girl is! She learned from watching the adults. Her resistance to any kind of teaching experience would have been increased by that understanding of the adults' "real" purpose.

QUESTION: *What about the point of view that discussions of sex with children in the lower grades break down their healthy sublimation, and excite them? This view maintains that sex education should be provided for at home, and that if a formal program of sex education is conducted it should be under the guidance of psychologically trained counselors, not by a teacher.*

DR. CALDERONE: Children are sexually and erotically stimulated by a large number of things. They can certainly find erotic stimulation in the advertisements. A recent *New York Times Magazine* ad carried one catchline, "What is the ugliest part of your body?" This advertisement is pure pornography. There is a black background with the photograph of an exquisite naked girl, sitting facing the viewer, her knees drawn up under her chin, and her arms and legs so disposed that the genitalia and breasts are carefully hidden. The printed words say, "What is the ugliest part of your body?" You must read the fine print to discover it's the feet! This kind of titillation is all around us. Look at the cosmetic ads, if you want to see a girl who is at the moment sexually stimulated. You can see it in her face, in the pout of her lips. This erotic stimulation is reaching the young subliminally. So, if in sex education courses the young can be learning something while they are being erotically stimulated (if they are!), you are on the black side of the ledger.

REV. UNSWORTH: Dr. Calderone, to oversimplify vastly—

DR. CALDERONE: Well, I am oversimplifying vastly, so we do share this!

REV. UNSWORTH: You are saying get there firstest with the bestest, because commerce and society are there now early with the worst. I think this is important, and maybe has something to do with the question stated earlier about the language that's used, and the idea of communicating not just facts but the *aura* of facts. I'd like to see more discussion about language in context. I could name, let's say, four or five terms for coitus used in different literary contexts which would range from the sacred to the diabolic in their aura. The word "fuck" was used in *Lady Chatterley's Lover* with an almost sacred aura, but in a Norman Mailer context it might well have almost a diabolical, dehumanizing aura. I wonder if part of our uncertainty about dealing with these matters is that we don't have any sense of the importance of language. Death and sex are both potentially sacred in their meaning, and this is why we have invented so many circumlocutions for both. We can make them ugly or communicative, depending upon the kind of language that we use. I am wary of allowing the street language of the youngsters to become our mode of communication with them, because the street language is often dehumanizing. It's a way of circumlocuting in order to be able to deal with sex in a "masculine," playing-field kind of atmosphere, which doesn't necessarily communicate bad values.

DR. CALDERONE: I agree with you. I think that it's the context in which we use the language—

COMMENT: When you talk about Norman Mailer or talk about *Lady Chatterley's Lover* you have to talk about Claude Brown and *Manchild in the Promised Land.*

DR. CALDERONE: Or *The One Hundred Dollar Misunderstanding!*

COMMENT: Yes. It is important to have a dialogue that makes some real sense, so that you are speaking the same language, but I don't think one can ignore certain language.

DR. CALDERONE: In spite of the fact that *Lady Chatterley's Lover* deals with an out-of-wedlock relationship, the relationship is somewhat sanctified by the fact that the husband is incapacitated. But that is not the point of the book.

REV. UNSWORTH: Or the point of that relationship.

DR. CALDERONE: Definitely *not* the point of that relationship, which changed from one purely at the physical level to a total one. Our young need to read with interpretation some books like that when they are mature and have been prepared. Now, they are going to pick up *The One Hundred Dollar Misunderstanding* on the book stand.

REV. UNSWORTH: It sounds like what any college student could write about a big weekend.

DR. CALDERONE: If he was perceptive. Now, you could discuss this book (which all the children will be reading anyway) in this context. The churches have to initiate open discussion within the context of *what is morality in a relationship.* Is it just going to bed with somebody to whom one is married? Many immoral, exploitative relationships exist within marriage. What is morality? Is it just somebody saying some words over a relationship?

QUESTION: *Regardless of what we may do, how we may go home and work our heads off to establish a program for better preparation, do you foresee the establishment of training programs in teacher training colleges and other colleges in sex courses?*

DR. CALDERONE: Yes, I do. This has already started. The University of Maryland has a large health education program. The undergraduates who think they are going to be teachers have a part of their work on sex education. Warren Johnson's excellent book *Human Sex and Sex Education,* is a fine one for professionals. The University of Connecticut at Storrs has another course. I see workshops being set up to which teachers can come for in-service training, with credits. This will be happening, but of course it can't all happen at once.

COMMENT: Well, there will be sacrifices, to a certain extent, until we have something like that.

DR. CALDERONE: You want to do something yesterday that should have been done fifteen years ago, so I think we are lucky if we get it done two years from now.

COMMENT: It seems to me that one of the strengths that independent schools have is that we can encourage, with relative impunity from public attack, free discussions especially in our literature and history classrooms, where one gets into values. The value connotations of sex are so likely to come up. You can hardly choose the book to read with an English class, once you get past the sixth grade, that doesn't involve these relationships. And it would seem to me that what all of us ought to be doing is to fill our classrooms with teachers who have an orientation toward free discussion and a kind of uninhibited approach to such matters when they come up in literature and history.

DR. CALDERONE: To move toward this in your schools you might have informal discussion programs among your teachers under some skilled leadership, which certainly you can bring in, with the same kind of meaning and insight you would like to have for the boys and girls.

QUESTION: *Do you get into discussions with the people who are responsible for the publications, distribution of magazines, the radio, the television, the mass media? They make the background from which our youngsters are getting their present view.*

DR. CALDERONE: Well, you would have to go to the top, because the little distributor in the small town takes what he gets, whether it's the movie, the television program, or whatever. But a culture gets in the mass media what it wants. Therefore, you are not going to get anywhere by dictating to anyone at the top. They still want to make money any way they can.

COMMENT: I heard a media leader say mass media will present what the public dictates, that there may be a long interim here where we are educating our young to demand different material. This applies also to our legislation—

DR. CALDERONE: —which about sex is benighted, punitive, and certainly destructive in practically all states. Illinois alone has achieved an almost model law regarding all aspects of sexual behavior, and this is to its credit.

REV. UNSWORTH: May I ask how many people in this room have among their parent bodies captains of industry, particularly in the mass communications media? (Numerous hands are raised.) Your job is outlined. In 1963, I opened the *New York Times Magazine* section to a bath salts ad with a woman in a bathtub with scrim over the lens. I said to my wife: "I make a prediction that in three years the scrim comes off, she's exposed in the rear, she's exposed in the sideview, and she's exposed face on, in that order." The ad on "the ugliest part of your body" fulfilled my prophecy. The people I just asked you to identify among your parents are the people who have created what we are talking about. They are creating the real form of contemporary prostitution. The only significant traffic in prostitution is now the traffic financed by these nice, decent people among your parent bodies—

DR. CALDERONE: Financed *and profited by*—

REV. UNSWORTH: Yes. I suggest that one task in sex education is to attack the problem of "decent" prostitution—and I would call it that. Prostitution is not a live business, really, nowadays, for all the obvious sociological reasons, except in this one form.

DR. CALDERONE: In 1965, Ernest Dichter, of the Institute for Motivational Research, predicted openly in the *Times* and the *Wall Street Journal* that advertising is going to become much more sexually open: "Toothpaste will be presented not only to make teeth whiter, but to make them stronger for biting, in passion."

COMMENT: We had a free discussion class for the seniors this year. We felt that the young people needed a chance to discuss freely their processes of growing up as people. I agree that this should be done in English and history classes as much as possible. Still, when you have a discussion group that is not for credit, not structured, is confidential and has nothing to do with students' college recommendations, you get a kind of discussion which you don't get in English or history.

Also, our students have asked for some exploration in modern dynamic psychology. We have to talk in terms of the development of a sense of identity, rather than just in terms of sex. What they really want to know is how to understand themselves, to understand why as girls they feel and think differently about experiences from the way boys do. And they want to know what the boys are thinking, what their roles are going to be. They need to have a place where they can be given the basic tools with which to make their choices, based on a sense of values, not just in the area of sex.

DR. CALDERONE: Remember Foster Doan said they had brought in the students from the neighboring girls' school for discussions on these things.

MR. DOAN: Those girls had some preparation first, as did our boys. They had a three-day discussion on what it means to be a woman. I don't know who led these—their chaplain got several people in the community to do it. We felt that what we were doing separately might be done better if we did it jointly.

DR. CALDERONE: How have those discussions come out?

MR. DOAN: They have been fantastic. We started off in a modest way, thinking maybe an hour or two might do it, that the boys and girls might run out, if for no other reason than from modesty, but they haven't. We have tried to keep the discussions as free as possible. We have not tried to structure the questions in any way. We simply allowed them to come out. Their teachers and ours have tried to stand on the outside and yet guide so the students don't go off on all sorts of tangents.

DR. CALDERONE: Is there any question that they don't want to ask when they get together?

MR. DOAN: We haven't found any yet. We have been—and my own modesty shows a little bit here—surprised and almost shocked by some of the questions and by the forthrightness. We have been delighted with it, I must say. One thing our school is going to try is to exchange chaplains. I am going over to the girls' school and their chaplain is to come to ours for some sessions. Perhaps some of these questions can come out.

DR. CALDERONE: I have found, with questions, that when there are no holds barred the boys and girls really have some! This is true when they know you are going to level with them, that you are not trying to run their lives or to make their decisions for them, that you are open to *any* questions. It is also important to identify those students who are having personal problems, and to give them a chance to have private discussions that might lead to counseling.

QUESTION: *Does it seem best at all levels to have these discussions on a coeducational basis?*

DR. CALDERONE: I once asked this question of a large high school system before junior and senior high school students. "How would you like to see a course set up?" What they said was reasonable: they decided that before junior high school the children should have all of the facts of reproduction. In fact, I am quoting them when I give this kind of recommendation. They then said that in junior high the boys and girls should have plenty of opportunity to be separated, but only if they wanted it for specific reasons. A lot of hesitancy has to do with a sense of delicacy and good taste rather than embarrassment about sex. They don't really like to ask certain questions in front of each other, although they would like to know. So, they recommended that they sometimes be separated in the junior high, but that they come together in the senior high.

QUESTION: *You made a statement that interested me tremendously when you said that males do not act "reproductively." Did you mean that* teen-age *males act sexually and not reproductively, or did you mean that intelligent, mature men do not give half a thought to reproduction?*

DR. CALDERONE: No, I meant this: In the act itself, how many men say: "I am now going to impregnate my wife, and have a baby, and become a father"? That is not what is happening. They are having sex. A woman has a twofold feeling about this. If she wants to go into motherhood and has had no particular fertility problem, her ability to respond in orgasm may be diminished because her anxiety to have sex in order to be impregnated is so great. So her *sexual* life may be somewhat affected by her *reproductive* life. I would say most of the sexual acts on the part of the males are probably sexually rather than reproductively oriented.

THIRD SESSION:
MRS. McINTOSH

My concern is with the problem faced by the school in working with its parents in the proper sex education of children. As I have already said, teachers do not operate in a vacuum; students will go home at night if they are in a day school, and will write home and return for weekends and holidays from a boarding school. What teachers and administrators say is bound to get back to parents eventually.

Our problem is a historical one because we are living in a transitional period. The rapidity of change in all phases of life in the twentieth century has produced a dislocation between the generations which makes proper communication between them intensely difficult. For parents who were brought up in a world which had Victorian moral and religious roots, interpretation and acceptance of sex changes is intensely difficult, regardless of their own conduct. In *theory* they still accept the moral codes of their own parents. Most teachers are in the same box; and what the school faces is the need to prepare their students to live in a world where values are confused and the usual guidelines are blurred.

Our first task is to understand—and to help our parents understand—the drastic changes that have taken place. We are indeed struggling between two worlds, one dead and the other striving to be born. The cataclysmic effect of two World Wars, a depression, a cold war followed by an uneasy peace, and our rapid technological advances, has revolutionized the living pattern of our families. Parents are faced with competitive pressures which absorb their attention and keep them preoccupied with materialistic goals. Their own convictions about the meaning of life have weakened, and in many cases their religious faith is gone.

Many negative forces, therefore, characterize the environment in which our students are growing up. Their parents are often unable or afraid to give them sophisticated, wise guidance. They then turn for their standards to their own contemporaries, to the books they read, the television they watch, the plays they see. Their goals are exploited by a highly organized commercial market. The ready availability of automobiles gives them a freedom never before known.

As Dr. Calderone has indicated, many PTA's in communities with fine public schools have become thoroughly aware of the dangers of the license given young people, and are at work on taking constructive action. Independent schools seem to be afraid to enter the lists; they have always counted on their parents to give proper standards. Now that the parents are as confused as the children, our boys and girls often go into college completely unprepared for the freedom they find there.

The colleges themselves have not been able to give much help. The report of the Group for the Advancement of Psychiatry, *Sex and the College Student,* gives an excellent analysis of the sex problems of undergraduates, but proposes no remedies. Moreover, it recommends no positive rule for college administrations in connection with the sexual behavior of their students. More and more the solutions seem to lie in the hands of the independent schools.

The only agents we have to work with are parents and teachers.

How can we help our parents to join us in a continuing dialogue on these important matters?

There is no need to be afraid of them. They are just as concerned as we are. It is a question of being able to interpret our concerns to them in ways that will make them see where we are going, and what we are trying to do to help their children.

Because I inherited a liberal school which has done a great deal from the point of view of sex education, we were able to have a series of classes, including a wonderful course in physiology and human reproduction, without too much backfire from the parents. And the backfire we had, we were able to cope with.

I would like to suggest that you have frequent parents' meetings in which you discuss exactly what you are trying to do, giving them a chance to tell you what their own doubts and difficulties are. This, of course, anticipates problems and does a great deal to do away with them. But it does not really solve them, because the problems are in their own lives. They have inherited the same inhibitions that our teachers have; the same puritanical repressions; similar desires to live a good life, but the same inability to articulate what makes it possible to live a good life. Most important of all is to bring fathers and mothers to the school together. Even boarding schools can have free communication with both parents through visiting days when the head can speak about the school's concerns.

What are the specific problems that we face within our schools, if we want to bring about the kind of approach to marriage and sexuality that Mary Calderone has been talking about? How do we get the benefits of frankness without the disadvantages of crudity; the benefits of clear, scientific teaching without losing the mystery and the unspoken values of sex and of marriage?

Courses in human reproduction and biology are, as Dr. Calderone has said, only the beginning. We have to count on our teachers in all subjects to reach out toward a larger concept. We must find ways of coping with the attitude that whatever you want to do is natural and human, and therefore is right. Contemporary literature and drama hammer this philosophy home to our young people; and we as teachers must find ways of raising the questions which will give our students the ammunition for countering their philosophy. Which action is better? What makes the better person? How does one create a good family? What is best for the girl as well as the boy? These profound questions must be discussed and answered if we are to fulfill our obligations to the young.

Certain other questions must be candidly faced. We have inherited in the East the British tradition of segregation of the sexes, and most of our schools are set up for boys or girls, with one-sex faculties. Does this framework adequately prepare young people for the real world? Our attitudes have changed somewhat in that many girls schools have men teachers—although I have not heard of any women on the faculties of the independent schools for boys. However, some of our oldest schools are now discussing the possibility of founding coordinate schools for the opposite sex, and some have actually taken this step.

What are our responsibilities in counteracting some of the negative influences of our time? We can't leave the morality of sex to the church. As educators, we must be concerned with the effect of modern sex approaches on married life and personal happiness. For example, what can we do about the deep impression made on students by the two Kinsey reports? As you remember, these were statistical studies of sex behavior of both men and women which were published in the late 1940's.

Most young people never read the reports themselves because they are very long and extensive. But the popular press and the women's magazines gave synopses and critiques which were widely read and discussed by college and high school students. The percentage of males and females who had sex experience before marriage, the statistics of those who practiced masturbation, and many other details about sex behavior and even perversions—all these passed into the consciousness and conversation of the young people, and the findings of the reports came to be considered norms for them.

The reports were discredited by reviewers and psychologists as representing weighted, self-selected samples. Most responsible doctors and educators discounted other reports and had no idea of their influence, direct or indirect, on the younger generation. I realize now that we should have taken them much more seriously than we did; that we should have insisted that studies be made of the effect on marriage and personality of early sex experience, especially for the girl. What kind of family does she create when she has had "affairs" before marriage? What does she teach her children? What happens to her and her husband when they have had intercourse as an engaged couple? The Kinsey report on women gave statistics which indicated that a woman who has had earlier sex experience has a quicker and more complete sexual response after marriage. But the report is concerned only with *physical* response; there is no mention in its index of love, children, family, happiness, self-fulfillment.

In the early 1950's James Pike was chaplain at Columbia and professor of religion. Mrs. Reinhold Niebuhr was chairman of our Barnard Department of Religion. They went with me to seek from the Rockefeller Foundation a grant to set up a project which would provide students with answers to the questions raised by the Kinsey reports. The foundation had financed the Kinsey reports. Mr. Dean Rusk, who was at that time president of the foundation, refused us the grant; and we three were never able to carry through our project.

What might the National Association of Independent Schools do in this area? What kinds of programs can we set up for our schools that will give teachers the opportunity to discuss human problems? How much can we expect of our teachers and exactly what can they do? Do you want them to give time out of their busy programs for counseling? Can we ask them to talk individually to parents and children? Do we expect them to seize every opportunity in their classes to bring in sex matters and discuss them with the group? These are the practical problems we are faced with in all our schools.

Our moral concern for these questions must express itself through our normal contacts with students. Many voices and influences in their environment are stressing the importance of physical experience and of sexual glamour. Young people must be given even greater opportunities to understand the qualities of character and personality that are the foundations of a permanent and creative marriage relationship. Teachers and administrators on both the school and college level must unite with parents in coming to grips with the sex problems faced by the younger generation; they must decide what they *themselves* believe and must be willing to share their beliefs. For example,

what do we think about premarital sex experience and what are
our considered reasons for our opinions? I have to confess that I
don't know what to answer to this question.

MRS. McINTOSH'S QUESTION PERIOD

COMMENT: Indiscriminately to expect faculty to take over the
responsibility for sex education and do it in terms of their disciplines (I like *that* part) could lead to greater difficulties than
those we now encounter. Dr. Calderone has said: "You have
to be discriminating. You have to know your faculty well
enough to know where the centers of possible new approaches,
of any approach, might be." But can anybody tell about faculty
seminars, or other ways of getting the subject introduced into
the faculty? The first step is not probably a big step. Nor is it
everyone that you come to and say: "We are going to talk about
sex, and here's how you do it." How do you identify what people in the faculty would have ability and aptitude for this?
How do you get a program going?

We are all in a position of having to start where we are,
knowing that this is belated. In one girls' boarding school, we
have as many styles and approaches for what we would like to
do as we have in ten or twelve different approaches to mathematics teaching. It's hard to know where and how to start. One
could do something fairly dangerous without meaning to, if
one doesn't know pretty well what an individual situation is.

We have tried to act in response to the girls until a formal
program, as such, is established. For example, bringing in
young house parents has met an enormous need. About five out
of eight of our young couples, each of whom has one or two
small children, have been requested to have seminars on various
aspects of all this. It's been gratifying to see the results. These
young people are picked carefully. They are graduate students,
most of them. Some are medical school interns. They are carrying a heavy intellectual program. They are idealistic. They
serve a purpose in helping the girls to see a fuller picture, including a family and dedication to something that isn't a material thing. It's good to start with, but it also makes a situation
in which the girls will ask their questions from—I hate this

term "subculture," but I am sure it exists—a subculture that we don't even penetrate normally. This is only a pitifully small start, but it has worked wonderfully well.

Teacher participation depends upon the teacher, certainly. It's a mistake to try to have every one of them do this. There must be something we have learned about finding some of the freest sort of thinking, which exists in the college communities that are the most highly intellectual. I find that our most high-powered teachers, to whom there is the greatest student response, treat all of these questions freely, because this is the atmosphere of the school. But many of them treat these exclusively intellectually, and with an intensity which is beyond the emotional experience of the girls.

COMMENT: The school administrators undoubtedly can figure out many good ways of getting a subject taught. You ask, "What do we expect of the teachers? Shall they counsel? Shall they give courses?" There are many answers and we can come up with those answers. But what is blocking progress is not any administrative or curricular difficulty. It's the difficulty of "the what" again. We all know that it makes a difference who teaches. I am not diminishing the importance of it, but I hope that we might get on to that "what." Many of us are hesitant not because we don't know how to administer but because we really don't know what we want to say at certain crucial points.

MRS. MCINTOSH: I think this is what was bothering that biology teacher I talked with. Suppose students ask her how she feels about premarital sex?

DR. CALDERONE: They will. That's almost the first question, to test her.

MRS. MCINTOSH: Then what will she say? Here is a community of parents around in the school, with the telephone *right there!* She doesn't know what to say.

COMMENT: I mentioned earlier that when Dr. Calderone came to our school she was enthusiastically received by the students and parents. We ran into one slight problem in some of our faculty, who were plainly shocked.

DR. CALDERONE: Why were they shocked? Because I did not answer *that* question categorically, but threw it back?

COMMENT: No, because you mentioned some of the so-called

wrong words. You were giving what some of them called a libertine approach. We've got some real Puritans. Anyway, we are planning a faculty conference before school begins which all the faculty members and their wives are expected to attend. We feel that to do anything about this issue our faculty must be able to *converse*. This has got to be the beginning, even before we get around to a formal educational program.

MRS. MCINTOSH: If you ever have a faculty meeting or a parents' meeting on this in a day school, it must be with the husbands and the wives. If the wives just come alone, your problem has not even begun to be solved.

DR. CALDERONE: What did I say that shocked your group? I certainly used all the proper words. I remember saying that we know a great deal about the various systems of the body, anatomically, physiologically, psychologically, and that we do not know much about sexuality for the simple reason that ours is a culture that is perfectly willing to smear sex all over the billboards and the communications media for profit, but is surprisingly unwilling to support honest scientific research about human sexual behavior. I remember saying that the Scandinavians think that we are an immoral people because of our hypocritical attitude which allows all sorts of petting at a very young age just as long as a girl remains a virgin, that is, the penis does not enter the vagina.

If I remember, the other shock was the first question: "What do you think about premarital sex?" I said: "What do *you* think about it?" And then I think I said: "What *I* think about it is essentially irrelevant. *You* are going to be the one to make the decision. . . ." Then I elaborated. If I did not make it clear, it is because certain faculty members did not *want* me to make it clear. They did not "hear" what I really said. They did not "hear" that I believe thoroughly in monogamy, but that premarital sex could possibly be an inconsequential question. It's only of the greatest importance if we make it so. I made it clear where I stood.

I met three professors of sociology recently and asked them this: "What do you think of monogamy?" They all came through with the most beautiful statements, based on their own marriages. I said, "Do you ever say this to your students?" They said, "Why, no, we don't." I said, "Why? Is it that you are afraid of appearing in an authoritarian light to the kids, and losing them?" They said, "Yes." So, I said, "Well, then, you are losing your best chance for selling something you really believe in." I think we have an obligation to make our own positions clear.

COMMENT: The school must be convinced first that this subject is really important. And then all these other technical matters about what we as teachers do about it will stumble or muddle along. We have had discussions of this kind, coeducational discussions, men and women, faculty members and outsiders, but we have only scratched the surface. An indication is this: I asked my librarian to make up a list of the books that dealt specifically with marriage and sex in our sixteen-thousand-volume library. I now have a list of twelve books! That's a fairly sad commentary on a coeducational school that has this opportunity. So, I think the question that I would have is, first, are we convinced that sex education is important enough so that we will undertake some kind of program to handle it? I think it is. Secondly, how to approach this? One of the best ways that I have found to start is to ask the seniors to read Farnsworth's article on "The Rational Approach to Sexual Morality," and some of the things that Mrs. McIntosh and Dr. Calderone have written. We then ask the students to comment on that reading. At least that starts the discussion.

Mrs. McIntosh's point about morality is essential. At a certain point the students always say: "What do you think?" I am not the slightest bit afraid to give my opinion, because they are asking for it. What they do with it I am not exactly sure.

COMMENT: The opportunities for developing insight among our faculties are not limited to the head-on collision between Dr. Calderone and the faculty and the students. For many years in our school, we had what we call clinical meetings in which each child was discussed periodically; and every one who met him had to be in the room at the time he was discussed. In that exchange occurred the chance for serving not only the best interests of the individual child, but the best possible mutual education of a faculty. It is one way to get at the problem of playing God, which is a temptation to any school principal. The head-on confrontation is far from the total aspect of the situation. Any forum within a school where there is frankness is an opportunity.

MRS. McINTOSH: I'd like to suggest about the forum and the confrontation that it's a salutary thing for boys' schools to get women to come in and for girls' schools to get men. I have had an opportunity to go to a number of different men's institutions, and it's rather touching to see the frankness of the boys in talking with me, because they want to ask me a number of very real questions. If you can bring a father into a girls' school, a man who has the knowhow to do this kind of thing, or who is perhaps a professional, or a mother who has the experience in this area and is good at encouraging discussion—this is sometimes a little easier than the formal lecture, though that has a great significance too.

COMMENT: I get the feeling that one of the prime ways of doing all this is through the faculty—and I think I share the concern that the faculty, at present, cannot do it. And I am not quite sure whether with a small involvement with Dr. Calderone and two or three others a year you are going to make authorities out of faculty. I just don't believe it. I think the problems are such, and the depth of knowledge is such, that I am not certain that the present faculty has the capacity, without going back to school for some long time, to handle sex education in the way that I would feel satisfied.

COMMENT: The administration needs to start having a little confidence in the faculty. No one expects the faculty member to be an authority. But it is our responsibility to see that everyone is trained, knows the facts, and doesn't himself have any horrible misconceptions to turn loose on students. I want my faculty members to discuss this openly, and answer questions. And if one is better than the other, so what? So are they in other areas. But I want to have confidence that the poorest one is at least informed, and is saying things that are not wrong. Then I can have confidence that the total faculty is presenting a wholesome picture.

COMMENT: I would like to say a word about this authority business, in relation to those sociology professors. There is something touching about this. In a lot of our schools there are essentially very liberated, very bright children, and very bright, liberated teachers. The teachers are afraid to sound Victorian. Then, they are afraid to make any statement which seems flat-footed: "This is what I believe." So, the teachers who really get to the students may be feeding them what they *think* they want to hear: "Anything goes. Let's not go on with this non-sense about what your parents or grandparents say." The stu-dents think this is supporting them, but they really want some-thing more specific than that. Again and again I have heard students condemn the teacher who won't say *anything* about what he believes, the one who will say: "Well, that's an indi-vidual matter," or "That's not my field," or "We haven't time to go into that now." And yet that kind of teacher thinks that this is the answer that is wanted; that this flatters the student; that the student should think: "Well, I must think this out for myself." We may all be too squeamish about giving our expe-rience or opinion when we have one.

COMMENT: Any school administrator who must depend on an in-spired maverick here and there to carry out these objectives is in a bind. You can get through to a faculty by holding so-called clinical meetings. The presence of a professional psychiatric or psychological person is a great catalyst. Without the psychol-ogist's perspective underlying issues may never be uncovered. I have had some experience with this in the town where I work. These various psychologists have had luncheon meetings with groups of teachers. A couple of schools have had team-teaching systems, and these teams met with a psychologist to talk not necessarily about sex education—although that be-came part of it—but about how they *felt* about their students, and about student behavior. With a trained, perceptive guide they were able to become pretty free in the course of a year of luncheon meetings, once or twice a week, about discussing their feelings. We began to get some of the underlying motivations for teachers' teaching in the first place: Why were these people there? What did they feel about children's behavior?

As for training, the whole field is in a bind in two ways. One, it has to start where it is; namely, that it has great numbers of teachers who are not particularly comfortable as these issues come up, and they have to be helped to become comfortable together—here's where you get the help of a psychiatric and

pediatric person. Two, the new teachers coming along are not
getting a great deal of training in this area in the schools of
education. The new teachers, who come into the independent
schools, if they are anything like me when I went into an independent school, haven't much training or experience in this
field.

COMMENT: The discussion of sex in our girls' school faculty
arouses a major anxiety among the single women on the faculty. They feel terribly uncomfortable about discussing these
things with the girls because they are afraid that the un-
disciplined imaginings of the girls are going to create for the
teachers a night life that will become upsetting to the daytime
teaching performance.

In some of our discussions the question of pedagogical trick-
ery came out. In throwing the question back at the youngsters:
"Well, what do you think?" there is a danger of students' in-
terpreting this as simply a trick, evading an honest discussion
of the issues. It doesn't apply only to sex, it applies to any other
area of the curriculum. These girls do want something more
than intellectual relativism.

COMMENT: I can't help becoming increasingly concerned when I
hear that we think we have to have the authoritarian approach,
or have the answers. This is where I think Dr. Calderone has
been most effective, by not projecting an authoritarian answer,
but by opening up exploration of what the result of their action will be, and how it will be accepted by society.

DR. CALDERONE: One of the ways in which we show our lack of
respect for the great qualities of our youngsters is by our un-
willingness to share our own uncertainties with them. These
young couples that were mentioned in the girls' school living
units are in important positions. They are no different from
anybody else. The fact that they are married does not mean
that they have solved all of their sexual problems. Indeed, none
of us ever solves all of them, because they occur as life goes on.

One of the most fascinating questions we could debate with
the students in a group that has had some preparation for it
is: "Do you still see marriage in our society, let's say twenty-five
or fifty years from now? When your children are your age, what
do you think will be the sexual patterns? What would you like

them to be?" We need to give parents a chance to sit down with teachers who can ask them, "What sexual questions have your children been asking you?" Gradually that could lead into their own uncertainties on how to act, so that they can be helped to understand the value of saying: "We don't know, but let's talk about it, and let's see what other people feel about these things. . . ." Until we can do that, I think we are not ful- filling our function as teachers.

COMMENT: When we talk about involving faculty and parents in our efforts, we are really talking about an involvement in life, particularly an involvement with the children. One of the ways to get teachers involved is to have them look at the raw product of their work—which is children, not subject matter. This can come about through counseling. Certainly counseling which involves not only the teacher but also possibly an administra- tor, a professional counselor, or a psychiatrist, is rewarding not only to the student but also to the teacher. We tried to institute some effort in our school recently. We did it without any pre- vious announcement to parents, children, or anybody else. We involved four faculty members in a lecture-type situation over a period of five weeks. In that time, we covered the gamut as much as we possibly could on this problem. The students were asked to take their questions back into the classroom. We didn't assign any teacher the responsibility of covering their questions, we just asked the students for their questions. The result was that the teachers *had* to face the issue, because the questions came to them in their own classrooms. What each one of us must face, whether we think it's the crucial issue or not, is that if the child asks us about premarital relationships we have to say something. What?

COMMENT: Coming from the school I have come from, I am sur- prised there is any other world except the Victorian one. We handle the problem of weekends by not giving them. We knew that boys were going through emotional crises. We knew that we were not equipped to handle these emotional crises. (This was not recognized until after I got out of school!) So we tried to decide what to do. And what we did was to get hold of a top university psychiatrist. The first thing that he did was talk about what he was going to do. He went into it in an interesting way by telling all of us just why we had chosen to teach in a boys' school. (He was a Freudian!) It slaughtered half of the faculty's interest in *anything!* What we do now, however, is have him come once a month. When a boy gets into an emotional crisis, those masters who are willing to *face* this psychiatrist—and who are involved in the life of the boy, whether on the athletic field, in the classroom, or in the dormitory—sit down and have a talk. Technically this man is simply trying to help the masters aid a boy who is in an emotional crisis. Naturally, he is carrying on a great deal of education, because in each case he usually tells a great deal about the psycho-sexual development of the human being, and he relates it to the masters' own fears in this whole area. As a result, the masters have a support in and are getting an education in this area which they might not take if they were confronted in a sort of classroom lecture situation. As I say, all this developed quite unconsciously on our part, because for eighty-five years our school hasn't admitted that sex exists!

REV. UNSWORTH: On the anxiety about the expertise of the faculty: it may not be unfair to say that this *does* reflect an administrator's concern for the political significance of what the biology teacher says about sex or what the history teacher says about sex, particularly in a day school, where the parent can pick up the phone and make your ear red because of an indiscretion on the part of the faculty member. We therefore expect to protect ourselves, administratively, behind the expertise of the faculty member. But if parents object to the faculty member's handling of the question of sex or politics we feel personally accountable, as administrators, for what that faculty member said. I think that is why this is a delicate matter in administrators' minds. I wonder if the problem of expertise isn't one closely related to what Dr. Calderone was saying, that *we have to share our uncertainties.* We expect all members of the faculty to be experts on certain general problems. They must all be experts on the significance and content of academic honesty. No matter what their field of teaching, they must all know what academic honesty means, how to interpret it, how to enforce it, and how to defend it before parents. That's really a problem of being expert in being human. Sex is another area where we are all required to be an expert in being human, and we cannot, any of us, be final experts in being human. We can only be expert to the extent that we *are* human, and freely human. Suppose we were able to adopt a posture with parents where we said, "Look, that faculty member is as human as you, no more, no less. I only expect him to be honest, be himself, and deal with this question openly. I don't expect him to present a politically acceptable posture." Maybe then we could satisfy parental anxiety.

QUESTION: *My school is an elementary day school. You said that in starting a program, and having a meeting with the faculty, it was particularly important in a day school to have faculty husbands and wives in on the meeting.*

MRS. MCINTOSH: And parents too—both fathers *and* mothers. This works well in college faculties; husbands and wives have discussions with the girls. One of the most effective ways of working with freshmen, for example, is to set up panel discussions, absolutely free-for-all, and to let the people say anything that they have in mind. For parent meetings, if you try to get across a message to your mothers in a mothers' meeting in the daytime, very often it arrives home in a rather strange state. I don't mean that the women are confused, exactly. It's just better if the men and women check each other. Maybe if you had the fathers alone the same thing would happen. They ought to have the chance to talk about it together.

QUESTION: *I am a faculty member. And I can't help saying that all of you who are administrators, I am sure, must know that your faculty, whether they want to say it to you directly or not, must experience a great deal of anxiety any time this topic of sex education comes up. But there is another area of anxiety. Faculty people are already quite concerned about your pressure on them in the academic areas in which they are directly involved. This rather than sex education is the big thing in their minds. And one of the questions that is going to come to you when you approach your faculty will be, "When are we going to do it? How can we afford the time?" I hear this question constantly in our school. What kind of answers are the administrators going to give their faculty members when the faculty say: "Look, we've got to get ready for that college board. They want to get into Princeton or Vassar or Smith. When do we do it all?"*

COMMENT: I visited a junior high English class not long ago where the children were discussing the Greek drama. You could not have a discussion of the Greek drama without getting involved in family relations and sexual mores! I feel you should not have another period with the English teacher where you talk about sex quite separately. A member of the faculty who tried to discuss the issues of the Greek drama without facing the family and sexual implications would not be a good English teacher.

Another point: Ours is a coeducational day school in the city, and we have children from age four to college. We believe that if we start with our guidance department in the nursery years, we will lay a good foundation, and prevent many problems from becoming acute. I am really making a plea for facing the fact that a great deal of good sex education can and should go on at preschool level, not only with the children but also with the parents and with the teacher. We have a psychiatric social worker in each school and a psychologist in each school. A psychiatrist comes once a week, not to work with the children but to confer with the faculty. And these meet with parents in groups. I know that the parents of five-year-olds, if we don't have a meeting, come with an S.O.S. and say, "Please help us answer the questions of our children." And they always fall into three categories. One is science—you know—"What makes the wind?" Second is sex, "What's the difference between boys and girls?" Third is death: "What makes people die and what happens to them?" The parents find all these questions difficult to answer, because they haven't thought out their own answers in many cases. So do the faculty find them difficult. We usually work with our guidance counselors, advising faculty and parents in answering children's questions, right from the beginning. So I am making a plea first to lay a foundation; then, while there will still be other questions as the students grow older, it will not be as difficult for parents, teachers and students to set up communications.

One other constructive, practical program that we have found in helping young people to develop a sense of responsibility for little children is having the older children work with the younger children. Beginning at the fifth and sixth grades, they help with the four- and five-year-olds. We give them an orientation course—again, with the psychiatric social worker, the nurse, and the pediatrician—in the dynamics of child development. We have films on why little children behave the way that they do, and on what some of their needs are. This has two values. It not only helps them in their work with the young children, but it helps them to understand themselves and their own siblings. Finally, there are camps in the summertime, and community projects, which provide a practical way of building a sense of responsibility for young children, without having to talk about it all the time.

COMMENT: All of us are borne down by some sense of guilt about our inability to talk honestly with the children. Perhaps we shouldn't carry this guilt. Having carried it for a bit, I wonder if we oughtn't to bury it, get rid of it. To feel guilty is not to help very much. I am not at all sure that to be *frank* is good enough either. The things I don't know are things that I've got to find out before I can honestly be frank with the children. There is so much technical information to absorb. We have to get hold of it or we are just stuck with "frankness" and an admission that it is not good enough. In other words, to be frank opens the avenue, but the avenues may run out into dead ends and perhaps may be even precipitous at the end.

COMMENT: If you carry this humble position too far, you will put us in a position of denying our sexuality as men and as women —which is the message that I keep getting from Dr. Calderone. A teacher could get so humble he wouldn't dare. We may find ourselves tending in the direction of finding our experts wholly amongst the guidance counselors, the churchmen, and the psychiatrists. These people are of tremendous value to us, but they should be recognized for their value in *supporting* all of us men and women in our effort to *be* men and women with the young. While none of us is expert—and we shouldn't pose to be so—still, after all, the only people who can talk about sexuality are men and women. The only difference between us is that there are those of us who can talk better than others. If we go too far along the "humble" path, we get back to the point where we are saying to our faculties: "You are the ones who ought to teach our children. You stand in front of them every day, and yet you can't teach them because you don't know enough and you dare not be so frank." And then, they are afraid that this is true—they know it's so—so they call in the expert. And the minute you start putting sex education wholly in the hands of the guidance counselor—and especially the psychiatrist—and the churchmen, you get trouble. You get the students hung up on the idea that "psychiatrists" means "there is maybe something about me that is about to be emotionally ill." You put it wholly in the hands of the churchmen, and "Here we go with the moral question again." By putting it in the hands of the guidance counselor you evade the point that sex really runs through all our subject matter. It can't be sifted out and put in a separate period. It's like teaching sacred studies once a week, whereas you have algebra five times. Then algebra must be five times as important as religion.

COMMENT: The reproductive material doesn't bother me. It's the moral and emotional area that is so sensitive and personal. We deal with adolescents at a time when they are terribly concerned about themselves, their relationships to one another and society, and we say, "Let's give them five different views and let them sift it out." I am not sure that this is good enough.

COMMENT: I think we are overestimating the knowledge and background that the average teacher has in this area. This is where a lot of our first efforts should be concentrated. Any teacher should have a good course in adolescent psychology, because it makes no difference how much you know about Latin, if you don't know anything about the learning processes and the emotional and physical problems of the child, you are not going to do as effective a job. I hesitate to get into this thing too rapidly, by turning the problem over to people who are inadequately informed and ill-prepared. Then, too, people interpret in the light of their own experience. It is difficult to do otherwise. Sex means one thing to you and an entirely different thing to me, as far as my physiological and emotional reactions are concerned. You have to be careful about who does the instructing.

COMMENT: In ten years as a dean of various sorts in a small men's college, I sat in on a once-weekly meeting of all the guidance people, the psychiatrist of the college, the chaplain, various teachers, which was entirely centered on case histories. We talked about the college boys. When I left to head a boys' school, I realized that this was maybe the most important experience that I had in those ten years, because I had learned so much about myself. It sneaked up on me. It was painless. And I realized that in the name of studying other people I had really learned a lot about myself. And I take it that the theme is, where do we get the help that we need to convey the information, to establish the rapport and the channels through which that information and that support and help can flow? We must draw upon our faculty, upon certain individuals that are particularly good, and upon the faculty as a whole, so that in their disciplines they can bring these things up, or rather let them naturally come up out of their disciplines. The real clue that we have to develop is that the case history idea may enable the faculty to become more knowledgeable and at the same time learn more about themselves, so that there won't be the threatening atmosphere we have heard described.

We ask, where do we get the help? We get it from the faculty. We need to do two things, to educate in straight subject matter, and reinforce the faculty member's awareness that it is okay *not* to be an authority. It is okay to be a human being. And it seems to me that we focus right on the idea of the case history as a way to dispel anxiety and learn something about personal relations.

MRS. MCINTOSH: I'd like to say just one last word. About five years ago the *Harvard Crimson* came out with a supplement in response to the baccalaureate sermon by President Pusey. President Pusey had told the boys the year before that in the old days there used to be a course required of all seniors, given by the president of the university, in moral philosophy. He had explained, "We couldn't have such a course now. It would be absolutely impossible to have it, because no one would agree as to what should be taught and everybody would think that what was taught was wrong." Then he said, "Your whole course at Harvard is a course in moral philosophy." A student wrote in the supplement: "We don't like to disagree diametrically with

our President, but *I* do, because the people who teach us will
express their opinions about the whole range of human experience and ideas *except* in moral philosophy. This is the thing
that makes us feel that our education at Harvard is inadequate."

The factual details are important, very important, and
should be correct. But I think it is our big job to enable our
teachers to have a significant relationship with the people with
whom they are in contact.

FOURTH SESSION:
DR. GUTTMACHER

I am an amateur. Dr. Calderone is a great professional at sex education. Mrs. McIntosh is a most distinguished pedagogue. I am neither. However, I am going to analyze the five questions I put to you earlier, and derive answers.

The first question: "Should we teach sex education in our schools?" The basis for my "yes" is multiple. Some of the recent college experiences I have had show the confused situation on many campuses. If the students had entered college with the type of education we have been talking about, or if the teachers had had this type of teaching when they were students, perhaps some of this confusion would not have existed.

In a large girls' college in one of our metropolises, I was told by responsible members of the faculty that they took it for granted that their students had had premarital sex. This college was close to a men's college. One of the problems was that this men's college had a good many students from Africa. The girls, in order to gain status and to rebel completely against their homes, consorted by preference with the African group. This compounded this college's particular problem.

At an airport an hour from a second college, I was met by two seniors, young men who told me that there was no provision made for dignified sex relations between the men and women on the campus. The college was totally uncooperative about this. Students were not permitted to have automobiles. And when students met in their legal little petting chambers, they had to keep the door ajar. Altogether it was a most undignified situation, and these young men wondered if I didn't think that the college ought to do something about it.

At a very fine girls' college I met with several hundred students, and then with smaller groups thereafter. It evolved that the peer reaction to premarital sex was that if a girl chose a single mate over a fairly protracted period, it was perfectly all right. She didn't lose status. She probably gained status in the eyes of her college mates. But when she was promiscuous, dating several men concurrently, she was ostracized. This was against the code of the particular college.

At a Southern university, I was asked whether I would meet with the vice president of the university, several of the deans, and an attractive and competent senior campus health physician. They told me *their* problems. One is that the temperature is conducive to a lot of outdoor activity all year round. The automobile is not barred on the campus, so that there are plenty of opportunities for students to have sexual relations, which they apparently have freely. There are problem pregnancies, and the college faculty group consulted me as to the college's responsibility in giving birth control advice to students. The college physician was very much troubled when a young woman of the college community came in to ask him for birth control advice, whether or not it was his duty to give her advice. They asked me to discuss this with them. The physician also told about venereal disease, which was not common in heterosexual relations but was particularly common in homosexual relations. I was so naïve I didn't realize this, but it poses a problem among men on some campuses.

Whether having meaningful sex education is going to lighten

the burdens of these colleges I can't be sure. But certainly you are surrendering students to the colleges very poorly prepared for college life, once they are given freedom from home. The question is, "How can we better prepare these students?" My belief is that good sex education might *un*confuse the student, might salvage some of them from serious difficulties later on. All of us who practice obstetrics and gynecology are constantly agonized by the young women who come with unplanned pregnancies, and by the tremendous trauma this causes to the whole family constellation: the girl, the boy involved, and often the four parents. When I was still in practice at Mt. Sinai, a young woman from one of the neighboring colleges came in and said she had been to an abortionist. Her problem now was an infected incomplete abortion. She was admitted to the hospital for treatment of the infection and completion of the abortion. I questioned the competence of the abortionist to whom she had gone. She told me, "Well, he is the man *all* of the girls of the college use." There is evidently an open bridge between this particular college and this particular abortionist. If I was ever naïve, I have ceased to be, through the interaction of all these situations. I call them to your attention because perhaps in your ivory towers, particularly when you teach lower school, you probably don't know the turmoil that the colleges and the college students are going through.

Mrs. McIntosh and I attended a conference which included presidents of women's and men's colleges. The interesting thing was that the presidents of the men's colleges had not the slightest interest or concern in the problems which faced the women's colleges in regard to sex on the campus. They said that they had enough trouble in maintaining ordinary campus discipline, the drinking in the dorms, the rowdyism, the panty raids. These were their primary concerns. They felt they could not be involved in what happened on the girls' campuses, even though one was located down the street, because their own indigenous problems overwhelmed them. It follows then that the girls' colleges are not to expect cooperation from the men's colleges in this matter.

I am just as troubled as you are about the attitude toward premarital sex. As you know, there is a minority opinion in American education that sex on the campus is no different than it was thirty years ago. I say quite strongly that *this is a minority opinion.* The majority opinion seems to be that sex on the campus is explosive, that it's quite different from sex on the campus thirty years ago. Is this good, or is it bad? I don't think that any of us can answer. Mrs. McIntosh quite correctly berates us all for not attempting to assess this in a scientific way. But I think it's too early. I think what we shall have to do is try to discover twenty years from now the divorce rate among our college youth who finished their colleges during this current period. How do they perform as parents? What has been their postmarital sex pattern, as far as fidelity is concerned? These will be the criteria by which we can measure the actions on today's campuses. Therefore I am unwilling to say that today's free campus sexuality is necessarily a bad development. It is, I confess, a confusing development. It is tough, certainly on all the administrators who have to live through it. It is tough on us parents, who see it in our children and in their peers. But I am not sure in the final analysis that it is necessarily going to be a destructive influence. I must leave open the question of what our attitude should be toward premarital sex.

With the uncertainty that I have in my own mind as to whether premarital sex is constructive or destructive, I think the ground rules that youth is laying down for itself are important. Many young people have concluded that a temporary faithful relationship is a good relationship, and a promiscuous relationship is a bad relationship. This shows selectivity, which is good, and it shows that they are thinking through this whole problem and not acting completely animal-like about it. They are thinking it through as intelligent human beings. Now, what is our responsibility? As I said when I started my Barnard discussion with the freshmen, I am in no position to moralize. I cannot tell young people whether premarital sex is good or bad. I feel it can be both a destructive influence and a constructive influence. It might be terribly destructive for many young people, particularly with the wrong people under the wrong auspices. On the other hand, it is perfectly possible that in certain situations it could be a constructive force. I tried to give these college women a feeling of what I term *sexual responsibility,* which simply means that they owe themselves consideration first of all. They have a deep obligation to their partner, but the primary consideration is themselves. They have to be true to the moral code which they have established for themselves, perhaps largely through their home environment. If they go against this, they'd have to realize that there might be a feeling of great guilt, a total dissatisfaction and a bad coloration for their whole sexual careers in the future. They should not impulsively give way, but they must think things through as deeply as they can.

I told them that sexual responsibility did not only mean wondering whether one should or should not have intercourse. It involved whether or not effective contraception was used at every coital exposure, so that they would not have the totally destructive experience of an unplanned pregnancy.

This, then, is not a moral code, perhaps, from your point of view. On the other hand, from my point of view, it is a practical moral position in the face of what I consider to be the values and attitudes of youth today.

I feel strongly that you in the independent schools must give leadership. After all, you don't have all the red tape to go through that the large public school systems have. You can initiate courses and instruction. You have to lead the way, not follow. Sex education *does* belong in your schools.

When I say sex education belongs in your schools I in no way imply that it does not belong as well in the public and parochial schools. The need for them is just as great and urgent. Every American child should have sound preparation in human sexuality, clear, frank understanding of the basic differences between the anatomy, physiology, psychology, and social roles of the male and female. Every child needs this education long before he leaves high school so that even in adolescence he may act with a prepared awareness of sexual responsibility.

Now, at what age levels should sex education begin? It is correctly said that sex education begins before birth of the child, and continues throughout its formative existence. Therefore, rightfully, it should be subtly and skillfully molded into the day-by-day curriculum of every class from nursery school on. But I am afraid that if you are going to depend on your fourth-grade classroom teacher just to bring it in by chance or to introduce it peripherally in social studies, a very incomplete job will result.

Everybody is going to expect the other guy to do it. The result will be that *nobody's* going to do it.

In the ideal situation you don't pull sex out of life, and say: "This is sex. Learn something about it." Sex is part of life. But unfortunately, I don't see any better way of doing it, currently, than by making a special exercise of it. Therefore you have to arrange your curriculum to include a specific entity, which you might call reproductive physiology, sex education, family life— I care not particularly what name you give it, but I do think you have to make this the responsibility of some teacher. When do you begin it? As we said, it should begin in the nursery school. I assume it does, but I don't think that you begin it in the nursery school as a formal teaching discipline. I would think, again, from my little personal experience, thanks to the Park School, that to begin the formal teaching in the fifth grade is ideal. If you are going to start formal sex education in the lower school, this is about the correct time to start.

I am much in favor of the physiologic approach, perhaps because I am a physician. I suppose each of us teaches according to his own background. But if you expose the child at this age to some simple physiologic experiments, showing the sexual differences between male and female rats, the spermatozoa of one, the eggs of the other, and the fetus in utero, these become terribly important and meaningful experiments to the children. There will be, I can assure you, no lack of questions.

Mrs. Guttmacher and I had an unforgettable experience in Stockholm three years ago. There is a magnificent Norwegian woman who started to become a physician. She had a laboratory accident which deprived her of several fingers of both hands, and she gave up medicine, moved to Sweden, and became a teacher. She is the marvelous and remarkable Mrs. Ottesen-Jensen. Mrs. Jensen has been the chief advocate of sex education in Sweden. We watched her give a class demonstration in a Stockholm school. There were a hundred and fifty teachers at the back and sides of the room. About thirty little boys and girls sat right in the center. This woman has, at the age of seventy-four, a completely electric personality, so that she immediately captured these children in a dramatic fashion. The first question she asked, after general conversation about the day and the coming of spring was, "Are any of you expecting a little brother or a little sister at your house?" About four hands went up. Then she said: "Tell me all about it!" And she was told all about it. Then she said: "Do you have any other brothers or sisters?" From there on she involved the whole group. They were the most excited eight-year-old children I ever saw. (They don't start school until seven, in Sweden, so it was the second grade.) She didn't introduce sex education with a microscope and a dead rat. She did it simply by questions and answers about dogs and cats, brothers and sisters, and other personal experiences of the children. She reinforced the feeling which I have so strongly that the teacher is almost as important, or even *as* important, as the content of the course. The student recognizes immediately when the teacher is uncomfortable with the subject. If you assign some spinster who has not thought deeply into this whole area to do the sex education at a certain age level in your classes, it's going to be an absolute flop. The man or woman has to be utterly comfortable with the topic. There must be no embarrassment. There is nothing that could or should embarrass them except pure pornography. Any question should be acceptable.

I remember once, in a public lecture to an adult group, I saw a hand waving wildly in the question period. I had called on everybody else, and finally this waving hand was the sole remaining, and I finally said, "Yes?" The question was, "Can you tell me what the Indian women wore when they menstruated?" Well, I couldn't care less, in the first place—and I didn't know, in the second place—and, what difference did it make? Yet I wasn't embarrassed. I simply said that unfortunately I was not acquainted with Indian folkways and therefore had to refer her to a greater authority. This is the kind of thing you have to do. You've got to be able to field all balls, flies or grounders.

Recently, when I was teaching at a private school, one boy of about sixteen said: "Dr. Guttmacher, tell me all you know about artificial insemination." So, I told him the basic facts about artificial insemination. Then one young girl wanted to know whether the egg always came from the same ovary, and we went into that. Then another child wanted to know how long the sex cells in the male lived within the body of the female, and how long after intercourse fertilization could take place, so we went into that. These are the kinds of questions that you get. I am talking much more about reproductive physiology than total sexuality, as this happens to be my particular area of interest and competence. Dr. Calderone talks directly about the sexual personality, the whole individual, sexual attitudes. I think I create attitudes in my listeners by my approach, but I am incapable of doing the same kind of masterful teaching job that Dr. Calderone does, for she views the topic in a far broader context than do I.

I am very, very happy to teach boys and girls together. I think to separate them at *any* stage in sex education is wrong, and I would take issue with anybody. One of the boys asked me something on menstruation yesterday in a coed class. I have never seen any inhibition about asking questions. It seems to me that you create a kind of pornographic aura when you feel you cannot talk about these things in mixed company, that you must separate the boys from the girls. I see no reason for this. On all occasions sex education ought to be taught as a coeducational discipline.

You have to repeat sex education several times in the curriculum because the focus is so different at the different age levels. When you are talking with eleven-year-olds you have a very different focus from when your class is for fourteen-year-olds and different again with a class of seventeen-years-olds. If you can teach these things at three different periods during the life of a student under your jurisdiction, it would be quite right and proper.

In your teaching at the high school level, you have to dig deeply into the whole anatomy of the world population problem. You have to discuss with students the various voluntary methods of population control and the hideous prospect that some generations in the future are going to be faced with, probably some kind of governmental population control, since we seem unable to succeed on a voluntary basis with any significant success. These young people are going to be our future leaders, and it is not too early, certainly at this age, to make them conversant with these problems.

At the age of seventeen, students need to be given accurate, detailed contraceptive knowledge. Sixteen or seventeen may be too late in some schools. Certainly if you were teaching in an underprivileged area, in your large slum areas, it would be far too late to talk about contraception to seventeen-years-olds. I would suspect that thirteen and fourteen is a much more logical age to talk about contraception there. But, for most of your groups, I think sixteen or seventeen is the proper time.

As to who should teach, I think any member of your faculty can teach sex education, except when it comes to such medical matters as contraception. You must have a physician well versed in the situation so that he can answer the questions with exactness and authority, so students really believe what he says. Even though your science teacher may have read all of the literature, he is not as well versed in the medical aspects as a physician. The physician needs, of course, a sympathetic attitude toward young people and an ability to gain their confidence. The physician is in a position to talk about such things as induced abortion and the problems which result therefrom, and other areas that may be of a much more medical nature than the regular part of sex education.

I have suggested for the "when" of sex education ages eleven, fourteen, and seventeen. I have given some insight as to what I consider the *content* should be. The content is tremendously different at these three age levels. Certainly at the fourteen-year-old level, you are talking mainly about adolescent boy and girl reactions, the area of masturbation, seminal emissions, and menstruation, things of this variety. When you get to the seventeen-year-old group, you are talking about many other things, including a good marriage and bad marriage, when to marry, and the whole area of contraception, population.

There remains the area of *teaching techniques*. These will vary considerably with the particular teacher. I have made it a personal rule never to use movies or slides. I like to draw on the blackboard because even though my drawings are crude I think I can carry my students with me much better than if I flash an excellent diagram on the screen. This happens to be a peculiar idiosyncrasy of my own. Drawing, more accurately blackboard scribbling, is a technique I feel comfortable with. On the other hand, you may get someone who can teach with movies most handsomely, plus colored slides, charts, and other aids.

About the value of a bibliography, that is, reading material for the student, I feel that most books leave unanswered questions. The best basic teaching is done not through the written page but through *confrontation*. You *face* your students. What you don't know you look up together. You may very well assign a topic to a student if a question comes up which cannot be resolved in class discussion. This becomes an excellent reason for research on the part of your student. In the main, I feel that literature is not nearly as useful as the give-and-take between students and teacher.

On *who* is to teach: I want to mention an interesting plan I have seen in a coeducational college. One speaker was selected to talk about the *physical* aspects of marriage, a second speaker the *moral and religious* aspects of marriage, and a third speaker the *economics* of marriage. They divided the student body into groups of twenty. Each member of the faculty, faculty wives, and faculty husbands were assigned to a group. Thus a group of twenty students met with one of the teachers or a teacher's wife or husband after each of the three formal presentations. If a group felt it had not completed its discussion after one or two hours, it was privileged to meet again and again at future times.

You have a tremendous resource in the spouse, the spouse of the teacher. You may find that the husband or the wife of your music teacher may be a darned good person to teach sex education to one of your classes. The fact that the person doesn't happen to be a member of your faculty does not deprive you of the great opportunity to use talent, if you have it in your school family.

Finally, I want to suggest that, in order to launch a program, it would be useful if the National Association of Independent Schools would set up regional workshops. Teachers who were going to have something to do with sex education in your schools would gather together for perhaps two days, to talk about curriculum and to see some model teaching for eleven-year-olds, for fourteen-year-olds, and for seventeen-year-olds, in well-arranged demonstration classes. We must have a standardized base line, and then stray off from the base line after the base is clearly laid and understood. Many of you are starting out without a base, and therefore you'll have to fumble. You are going to save yourselves a lot of fumbling time if N.A.I.S. sets up these regional conferences with well-qualified persons to meet with teachers and talk and plan with them. Look in your communities—there may be somebody doing an awfully good job teaching the eleven-year-old or the fourteen-year-old. Get such a person to meet with you, and work plans out together. Our motives are magnificent in an effort like this. We have nothing to gain except a highly instructed student who hopefully can approach sex life away from the shelter of the home with much more confidence and competence.

DR. GUTTMACHER'S QUESTION PERIOD

DR. CALDERONE: It's instructive to note that the Swedes are dissatisfied with the results of their own sex education program. They find they have been too fact-orientated. They haven't taken into account ethics, morals, spiritual values enough. They find they have really been doing reproduction education, not sex education in the larger sense that we're beginning to understand. So they have a commission that is re-examining the whole program at the Swedish schools.

COMMENT: I don't mean to be frivolous about this, but I sometimes think that if we can find out why somebody else seems to know more than we do, perhaps we might understand more about our own ignorance, and know better which way to proceed.

DR. CALDERONE: I don't think they do. I don't think they feel they do.

DR. GUTTMACHER: They have a different attitude than we do, a much franker attitude, certainly. For example, they look upon premarital sex differently from the way most of our people look upon it. In many areas, the Swedes are more liberated. They are also dissatisfied. They have had a lot of things going wrong. Even though they have moderately liberal abortion laws, they still have a fairly high incidence of illegal abortion. They have illegitimacy, though perhaps not so commonly as here. At any rate they are not happy with the results they are getting. Everybody is fumbling in this area. Their achievements are not nearly equal to their goals. Isn't that true, Mary?

DR. CALDERONE: That's true. And we should realize that they are not as all-permissive as we seem to think they are. In fact, the

Swedes look upon *us* as more permissive than themselves because our society apparently countenances petting, sexual experiences in the very, very young, to mutual orgasms, whereas in their society the children are not encouraged to single-date nearly as early as in our society.

Although 95 percent of their women are supposed to have had sex experience before marriage according to some of the studies, the fact is that they had them with one, possibly two men. They were part of a premarital commitment, and the experiences did not happen until the late teens, in general.

It's a different kind of atmosphere.

COMMENT: I once heard a professor from the University of Stockholm say, "We do in the bedrooms what you people do in the parks. . . ." That was his answer to that comment about how the Swedes are supposed to be so promiscuous.

COMMENT: This "Scandinavian point of view" is a lot on the minds of our seniors. They think everything seems to be working out very beautifully in Sweden. They aren't talking about the promiscuity, either. They are talking about the one or two occasions of relationship before marriage.

DR. GUTTMACHER: I am no authority, but I have talked to Mrs. Ottesen-Jensen. She is quite enthusiastic about their attitude. The Swedish government has published guides on sex instruction at the various ages and grades, with the content of the course for such ags groups.

Of course the weakness is that it is legally necessary, in theory, to give sex education in every class, every year, but very often teachers slough it off. They don't do it because they feel uncomfortable with it. That's why there were a hundred and fifty teachers to watch Mrs. Jensen teach the eight-year-olds.

DR. CALDERONE: You can write to the Swedish Information Service, New York City, and get an excellent pamphlet by Birgitta Linnér. She's a Swedish family counselor. It's called *Society and Sex in Sweden*.

QUESTION: *It has been my understanding, and I wonder if there is any scientific backing for it, that the sexual freedom in Scandinavian countries, particularly in Sweden, is quite different as between the sexes—it's much freerer with the female than the male. Is that true?*

DR. CALDERONE: Well, I'll give you the answer that Dr. Kerston Alkin gave; that is, there are two kinds of girls in Denmark. There are "Danish" girls and then there are what are called the "American" girls, the Danish girls who have adopted the American patterns, principally learned from American sailors. Again, this is *not* a permissive culture. There is a real resentment of advances from American males because the girls have been brought up to believe in sex with commitment to one person in anticipation of marriage. This stems from the old Lutheran tradition, in which the betrothal ceremony was a sign for sexual intercourse, and the marriage ceremony might not be performed until a child was on the way.

REV. UNSWORTH: It is particularly important, in relation to the Scandinavian countries, to recognize the necessity that we feel to mythologize cultures like the Swedish and Danish culture. It is like the middle-aged people who mythologize what goes on on the college campus, in part because they wish it had been going on when they went to college.

DR. CALDERONE: Or they wish they were still young enough to give it a go!

REV. UNSWORTH: Or that they were still young enough to enroll! Dr. Calderone is talking about the accelerator and the brake pedal, and the middle-aged people are wondering why they weren't there to buy a license! There is a great deal of mythologizing about this sort of thing. The first answer has got to be: "Do you know what you are talking about? The second answer is precisely the one just given. The Scandinavians are interested *not* in premarital sexual intercourse, but in monogamy. They are less precise about when one form of sexual expression is permitted than we are. We suffer from a cultural disease of being preoccupied with technical virginity, which is part of a larger social disease of isolating the parts of the human body, and the physiological sexual act, from the sexual being.

QUESTION: *Here it is again: What are the schools responsible for teaching? We have been accused of diluting our curriculum, of taking over the function of the family and the church. Society, through its agencies, has been flunking sex education. The schools are undertaking it. But we are precipitating another round of accusations about the school's responsibility and about dilution of learning. We should be able to help parents grow as parents. But at the same time we have to face the issues of whether we are taking unto ourselves more than society will permit without challenge.*

DR. GUTTMACHER: The alternative is, if you don't do it, will it be done by anyone else? Or will it fall by the wayside? This is the dilemma we are in. If you surrender it to the parents, the task undoubtedly will not be done. If you surrender it to the church, then it's done in part—not everybody is church-connected. But also, with due deference to Reverend Unsworth, there are a lot of ministers who approach this thing as a purely moral issue and who come down pretty heavy-footed on the whole thing. That would destroy any interest or any confidence that a child might have.

You say you are putting a burden on the school, but is there something or somebody who can take this burden off the schools? Or should the child remain untaught, except by his peers? As far as I can see, you are only going to have three choices: parents, ministers, or peers. I see none of them as satisfactory, therefore I think the school has to do it.

QUESTION: *What about the role an independent school can play in the mobilization of community opinion?*

DR. CALDERONE: I suppose it's the same kind of leadership role that any other group might assume, if it wished to, such as the Medical Society—I have seen it happen there. P.T.A.'s have taken leadership in some communities or a group of clergymen in others.

I went down to Tulsa, Oklahoma, for a meeting, sponsored by Father Charles Johnson, of the Catholic Information Center. Through him I met with the clergymen of all denominations. Now who takes the leadership? I don't think it is important. But it *is* important not to *retain* the leadership. In some areas, I have advised Planned Parenthood Centers, as I do anybody else, not to retain the leadership. *Involve all the other elements of your community equally with you.* Otherwise, somebody is going to be in a position of appearing to force something down a community's throat which the community is not ready to accept.

REV. UNSWORTH: I would like to suggest that the best way for the independent school to fulfill this responsibility is to go ahead and do it. As with most points of critical change in society, it is not until somebody goes ahead and does something that the rest of society wakes up to the fact that it must be done and that it's long past due.

The Supreme Court went ahead and "did it," and the schools caught up. Churches came trailing along a little later. Now some of the rest of society is catching up with the question of integration.

You have a freedom to go ahead and act. You also have the resources.

DR. CALDERONE: And the *human* resources, as well.

COMMENT: Remember around 1940, there was a strong movement among the schools, public and independent, to restructure our whole society. The great book of the day was *Dare the School Build a New Social Order?* And, the minute an effort was made, the organizations faltered, and some of them died. The faculties of the schools were not competent to structure a new social order. We are still undertaking something which the community must be persuaded we are ready to deliver.

DR. CALDERONE: It seems to me that the whole function of our meeting here is not to give you any information that you didn't have already, or didn't know darn well where to get. It was just simply to open the door and say, *"Yes, you can."*

COMMENT: We can't change the whole face and attitude of the nation. But we *can* begin where we are.

DR. CALDERONE: Well, that's what we are all doing. The private schools are in a different situation from the public schools. The public schools derive their funds from public moneys and therefore must have public acceptance. It is essential that they not proceed any faster than their own particular local public is willing to have them go. The private schools are in a particular position of being responsible only to their trustees, to their parent bodies, and to themselves. Therefore, you can have the opportunity of a real leadership job.

QUESTION: *You spoke of an explosion in sexual matters. Is it imagined that the right program of sex education will cause this explosion to cease or to diminish?*

DR. GUTTMACHER: No. I don't think that the libido has changed from one generation to another. I think the *expression* of the libido has changed. In the generation previous to the current one sexual relations between boys and girls were to be expressed but not to the extreme of sexual intercourse. And the modern generation thinks that the attitude of the previous generation was crazy. Why? They feel that they are realists. They are skeptical. They don't take the myths that we try to give them, that "everything is okay up to a certain point, and beyond that you dare not cross the bridge." They just can't see any kind of realism in this kind of thing. They are leading life in a much more down-to-earth fashion than the previous generation.

I don't think that petting has changed. There was just as heavy petting thirty years ago as there is today. Maybe there is more of it because of the automobile, which has changed a great many of our sex ways and many other folkways. The change has been from the living room to the automobile, a much more private and available place. When I grew up as a young boy and man in Baltimore a half century ago, we knew there were only two types of girls: the girl who submitted to total intercourse and the one who didn't. The one who did got noised around by the group. In those days, some parents thought sex was an absolute safety valve. On Thursday nights, a lot of the boys in our neighborhood got $3 and went down to Pearl Street, our red-light district, sometimes accompanied by their fathers, because this was the thing to do.

There were a good many of us who revolted against this idea, Sir Galahads who thought that this was wrong, who put women on a pedestal. In those days you never attempted intercourse, because you knew you couldn't have it with the girl whom you dated, and you didn't want to avail yourself of the only other opportunity.

Times have changed so much that we've wiped out the red-light district completely. We have a single sex standard. When I grew up we had a double sex standard, and we grew up quite happily this way. The boy could do anything, the girl could do nothing. Now we have wiped this out, with the emancipation of the woman. She wants equality of treatment. So we've changed the whole attitude toward sex. Single dating is another new phenomenon. In my generation, when you took a girl to a dance, you were lucky to be able to dance half a dance with her, because she wanted everybody to cut in on her. The girl felt the point of the ball was to leave the dance with her program all scarred over with half dances. Today, when a girl goes to a dance she goes with one guy and dances all evening with him. We are forcing our children into a totally different type of relationship. Now as to what we are going to accomplish in sex education: I hope we will take away some of the confusion in the minds of our children. They don't know nearly as much about their reproductive physiology as many of you *think* they do. They see sexual material in all of the media. They grasp only part of it. The questions that they ask sound silly sometimes, because they should know the answers themselves, but they obviously don't. So, number *one,* we can give them some factual information. Number *two,* we can try to help them to be sexually responsible, to themselves primarily, to develop their own code and follow it. Then if they decide that premarital sex is part of their code, they've got to protect themselves—and the girls who are their sexual mates.

These are not vague ideals. Our efforts should equip young people to have a less traumatic existence in the outer world and to have better marriages. One out of six brides in America is pregnant at the time of marriage; two out of five *teen-age* brides are pregnant at the time of marriage. A hell of a lot of marriages are forced. A lot of college educations are scrapped because the choice is, "Shall I marry the girl, or shall she have an illegitimate child, or shall she get an abortion?" The boy marries the girl, he has to leave college, he becomes a thwarted lab technician for his whole life instead of becoming a professor of theoretical surgery at a great medical school. Or the girl becomes an educational dropout, a step she is likely to regret bitterly her whole life. Furthermore she is likely to be resentful of the male who in her mind bears all of the responsibility.

These are tragedies. There is nothing quite as tragic in youth today as an interruption of a fully planned college intellectual career, simply because a family is impetuously forced on these young people.

COMMENT: Speaking as a doctor, I am part of that minority opinion that considers that sexual practice hasn't changed as much on our college campuses as it's reputed to have done. What has changed more drastically is the *attitude* toward sex, the openness with which sex is discussed—the scrim that has come off the lens. This is what makes it so important to discuss sex in the secondary schools, to bring into open discussion not only *reproductive* activity but *sexual* activity, as Dr. Calderone makes the distinction, and in relation to a moral and psychological background. I don't see that any of our younger generation is going to accept a moral standard which is imposed by anyone else, but a discussion of it, either in personal terms or in medical terms, can be useful.

I just want to record my personal opinion, not only as a doctor but as a parent of two boys who will be in a secondary school shortly, that it is a responsibility of the independent schools to deal with this subject, and deal with it as a part of health education in general, as Dr. Calderone suggested.

I was talking to a teacher earlier urging him to introduce a formal course in health education in the tenth, eleventh, and twelfth grades. It doesn't have to be a course which brings the students right up to the frontier of molecular biology or some esoteric field of history. The secondary school curriculum shouldn't be completely discipline orientated. Certainly health education can't be purely discipline orientated, which is just the problem it runs into in the prestige colleges. We need to bring students to the point where they will carry on their own education. In health education, this is doubly important, because they are not going to be able to get anything more in college, and yet they should be able to keep up with what is published and not be like one of my graduate students a couple of years ago, who thought the kidneys ran into the intestinal tract.

REV. UNSWORTH: Dr. William MacNaughton gathered some facts about the change in attitudes among young men through their four years of college on whether or not sexual intercourse was permissible, and, if so, under what conditions. He also explored their attitude toward the permissibility of sexual activity for women of the same age. His findings can contribute much to this discussion.

DR. MACNAUGHTON: A lot of the boys whom we would see in our

counseling in college would be coming from schools similar to those represented in large number here. The attitudes revealed among freshmen, and then four years later among seniors, are not likely to surprise you, in that they represent a very wide spectrum of opinion. The questions were purposely designed to leave the student a lot of latitude in answering what had to be an objective questionnaire. There are a lot of reservations I have—and I think you all would have, on examining any sociological data of this sort. At any rate, before they had any contamination with upperclassmen or even each other, students on entrance to the men's college where I did the study were asked to answer a questionnaire the first day. They completed another questionnaire late in the spring of their freshman year, and finally at the midpoint of their senior year. The survey encompassed a lot of attitudes not related directly to sexual ones. But, regarding the questions that you are especially interested in, we found that there was a liberation of conservative attitudes in the direction of students' being much more permissive not only in what they would expect as seniors (compared with what they expected as freshmen) but also in terms of their peer behavior, their own perceptions, and their own changes of attitudes over the four years. Students who held what used to be called traditional morality points of view—that is, no intercourse before marriage—abandoned that point of view in overwhelming numbers, and became, at least on paper, relatively libertine.

Again, you cannot be sure that what they are saying on paper is what they would feel in their hearts at all times. Interestingly enough, in relation to Dr. Guttmacher's remarks on the double standard, there is ample evidence in this study and in others that some college men still expect more reserved, inhibited sexual behavior on the part of college women. To these students acceptable, understandable behavior on the part of girls at the college age meant that women ought to behave more discreetly, ought to have fewer affairs, ought to be more discriminating in their choice of sexual partners.

DR. GUTTMACHER: Did they speak of chastity for their future wives?

DR. MACNAUGHTON: Fifteen years ago a study asked this question, and we lifted that question verbatim and used it. In the fall of freshman year, when asked whether, if they found that the girl to whom they were engaged had had previous sexual relations, they would break the engagement, 6 percent of the students said, "Yes." The responses which were flat "No" went this way: freshman fall, 40 percent; freshmen spring, 49 percent; senior year, 76 percent.

The "uncertain" responses took an interesting drop. In the freshman fall, 53 percent were uncertain; in the freshman spring, 47 percent; in the senior year, 22 percent. That suggests that those students who were ambivalent about this kind of response shifted by the senior year almost invariably in the direction of increased permissiveness.

This included 100 percent sampling of the class of 1965. In the fall of the freshman year, 805 students answered the questionnaire. Then the number dropped according to attrition. It's an unusual study in that we did sample the entire population of our freshman class.

QUESTION: *Are there any figures that would throw light on young men's attitudes toward acceptance of permissiveness in the behavior of their sisters, as contrasted to other people's sisters?*

DR. MACNAUGHTON: The question hasn't been asked just that way, to the best of my knowledge. I think we'd all have hunches as to what the answer would be under those circumstances, but frankly I don't know of any figures that would back up our hunch.

COMMENT: One study shows that even while *attitudes* are getting much more permissive, the *amount of sexual activity* is much less than is talked about by the students reported on in the study.

DR. CALDERONE: At the Grove Conference, the sociologists were generally in agreement that the change has not been particularly great in the college age. Where the change has come is in *the dropping age level at which full sexual activity is beginning,* and this was our concern.

REV. UNSWORTH: Observing college seniors for the last fifteen years, I would say the only significant difference now is that a higher percentage of college students do have full sexual exposure and experience before marriage than was the case fifteen years ago.

QUESTION: *These figures reinforce the importance of Dr. Gutt-*

macher's statement that some instruction on contraceptives should be given to both sexes, though it is particularly important for the girls. You mentioned age seventeen as being the time when this type of instruction was desirable. I did not hear or see a sigh of relief go around the circle, but I felt one. Most of us are affiliated with secondary schools. By seventeen, our students are on the point of graduation. Our schools can leave it to somebody else to do this if they want to. For those who don't *want to leave it to somebody else, do you have any suggestions, Dr. Guttmacher, on how you introduce this material, including data on contraception, into the curriculum of a school?*

DR. GUTTMACHER: It's part of what we call sex education, or reproductive education. It's such a necessary part and such a logical part of the instruction. I meet with sophomores and seniors together in the secondary school I spoke of earlier. They ask for the facts, which I try to make clear to them. I feel no reticence in this. It's such an important and logical thing to think out, whether they are going to use contraceptives or not. You have no fear of being misunderstood when you say: "I don't think you should do this. But, if you are going to do this, this is the way you ought to protect yourself."

Now, I'd like to get back to the problem which faces you and your school physicians less perhaps than it faces the college physician: the responsibility of giving birth control advice to students. This dilemma faces me on every campus to which I go. My advice is that a college physician is under no obligation to give birth control advice to students on the campus, because there is an unwritten contract between the parent and the college, and in this contract the parent does not expect birth control information to be included by the college physician. On the other hand, the college physician cannot throw the boys and girls to the wolves: what he has to do is set up a panel of local physicians to whom the girl or boy can be sent. *They* can treat the girl or boy just like any other member of the general community who comes in and seeks medical advice. Most physicians will give birth control advice to unmarried people if they feel it's wise and proper. I have never yet had a virgin come to me to seek birth control advice. The young people had already made up their minds and have had sexual intercourse before they came. Therefore, advice from me was pretty damned important. I doubt that many girls come to the physician *in anticipation of intercourse,* before they make the decision. They usually come to you after the decision is made and intercourse already practiced.

On that basis, it is highly important that the college do something. The college has thus relieved itself of its responsibility to the parent and to the student: the doctor in the community has to make up his or her mind whether this particular individual is qualified to receive birth control advice. He doesn't have to give it to anybody. He can say that he is not interested in giving the advice, and just say he is sorry, they'd better see someone else. More often than not, the information is necessary, and we should give the individual the kind of information she needs. But this is a hot potato for the colleges. It is not an easy decision to make.

I am sure such situations present themselves to physicians and other faculty members of secondary schools, perhaps more frequently in slum areas. In one recent year eleven hundred female students had to drop out of the public city secondary schools of New York City because of a diagnosed pregnancy. Add, too, those who escaped detection through either induced abortion or the convenient onset of the summer holiday. If before pregnancy had begun they had come to the school physician for help, what would he have done? I fear, nothing.

DR. CALDERONE: The decision to have sexual relationships is a personal and private decision. The burden of the decision is on the individual. And, in the same way, to support this decision, the decision of seeking contraception should also be a burden placed on the individual. But young people should be given all information and known *help to make a good decision.* Where this applies under the legal age is another problem.

This is a special question to physicians.

REV. UNSWORTH: The problem of giving advice and guidance on contraception are complicated, of course, and many college authorities are trying now to devise policies which will meet the needs of students, the legitimate desires of their parents, and the requirements of law and social custom. As you can imagine, these things are not always easy to reconcile, so a college counselor needs a combination of wisdom, sensitivity, and practical policy. Whether a college encourages the dissemination of contraceptive information or forbids it, student attitudes and destinies are bound to be affected.

What we must avoid in this matter is a situation like the one we now have in relation to the use of alcoholic beverages, which is illegal for three-fourths of most undergraduate bodies, but practiced by that many or more underaged students with the college's tacit permission. The resulting hypocrisy undermines moral integrity on all sides.

DR. GUTTMACHER: What do you think the colleges' responsibility is in this area?

REV. UNSWORTH: I think your approach is the one I would want to follow: that is, assume that the college cannot take to itself the responsibility which is the domain of the parents.

DR. GUTTMACHER: Unless the parent requests it of the college.

REV. UNSWORTH: In that case, the parent must make the request of an individual doctor, as a physician, and not of the college as an institution with a policy. Putting a patient in the hands of a doctor for this purpose is like putting the patient in the hands of a doctor for any other purpose. It's up to the doctor to decide whether he wants to ask other doctors to come in on the case, or whether he wants to handle it himself, as a physician.

QUESTION: *If I hear you correctly you are saying that the secondary school should* not *give out contraceptive advice to its students. If it's a hot potato for the colleges, what in the name of heaven is it going to be in secondary schools?*

DR. GUTTMACHER: When I talk to secondary school students, I talk theory, and not to an individual case. I explain how various contraceptives work. I don't go into the minutiae that one goes into in the private office, between patient and doctor. In a school classroom you are not writing out a prescription. You talk about the mechanical methods, what they are and how they work. It is certainly true that after a student has heard me talk he or she is very *ill*-equipped to practice contraception. They must get medical advice. I am not doing this as I would with a patient in my office.

DR. CALDERONE: I am afraid that if you really do your usual good job of giving information on contraception, the student will know that a condom will practically insure them 100 percent protection. They will know that they can buy this without any prescription. But they will probably know about this anyway. We have had articles in the big magazines. For years Catholics have been able to buy the rhythm books. Kids get them from Sears, Roebuck by saying they are married. That doesn't mean that any of us would agree that we should go so far as to see to it that girls in schools should be given contraceptives. This, I think, is a total responsibility of the parent.

QUESTION: *What about that article in the* New York Times Magazine *section about a morning-after pill? If you can bootleg LSD, I am sure you can bootleg those pills.*

DR. CALDERONE: Well, it's still a private decision. The school cannot put itself in the position of participating in the act of providing contraception.

REV. UNSWORTH: That is true.

FIFTH SESSION:
REV. UNSWORTH

It's now time to turn to questions of framework—that is to say, questions concerning the moral values, the moral structure, within which we want to speak about sex, sexuality, and sexual responsibility with our young. You live, whether you know it or not, in a society that sells *Playboy*. This is the most representative magazine on the American scene as regards sexual attitudes. If you want to find an explicit, unvarnished statement of the American ideology of sex, I recommend *Playboy*. It says the following things:

1. Sex is slick.

2. Sex is male. Female sexuality doesn't exist in *Playboy*. Females are the *object* of sexuality. They are not themselves possessed of sexuality.

3. Sex is an aspect of the good life, along with clothes, gourmet food, sports cars, and the other material benefits of an affluent society.

4. Single sex is free. Experimentation with it is good and ought to be encouraged. Liberation of attitudes in conduct and behavior is a good thing.

5. Marital monogamy and marital fidelity are absolute and unchallengeable ethical commitments.

A final parenthetical observation: Hugh Hefner is single, he eats hamburgers and drinks Pepsi. Hugh Hefner is single, therefore single sex is free and experimentation in it is good. Marital monogamy is absolute, therefore stay away from it. That's the implicit value from *Playboy*. Marriage is to be feared. This last statement is a value statement that American society makes. It makes it explicitly in *Playboy*, but it makes it all over the place elsewhere. The *New York Times* ran an article in its magazine section some time ago on the ten most popular TV shows. In *none* of those ten most popular TV shows was there a significant marriage relationship portrayed. The possible exception was the Dick Van Dyke show. But any man in his right mind who thinks he is going to marry Mary Tyler Moore and live a life like the one Dick Van Dyke lives with her on TV is out of his head! The ten most popular TV shows early in 1966 were based on either divorced persons, widowers, widows, or single persons, but in no case around the drama and the possibility of the richness in a permanent relationship, a marriage relationship.

This is a much more fundamental sickness in the society than anything having to do with premarital coitus or premarital sexual behavior. The question is permanent relationship. Do we believe in sexuality and its fundamental meaning? Are we mature enough as a society to affirm sexuality as one of the means by which lasting, enriching human relationships are established?

You deal with students at a stage where you may have some effect on their apprehension of the society. You may be able to help form their values in contradistinction to the values of the society. You may be able to warn them to resist the signals which are coming at them from all sides, and which suggest that sex is nothing more than fun and games. It seems to me the two key value questions that have to be tackled when we talk about a framework for sex education are *marriage* and permanent relationship and *commercial prostitution of sex*.

These are the key questions. In response to them, I have some admonitions. (A preacher always has to have some admonitions!) Have some faith in the value decisions of the young, and in their capacity to make them. They sometimes make better ones than we do. A while back a president of a fine college wrote an article which appeared in a major magazine on the changing habits of dating, from the time that he was in college in the twenties to the time he wrote the article in the fifties. The major change, he said, was away from the habit of dating many girls, keeping many relationships going, each of them designed to fit certain occasions, one for the opera, another for the beer hall, another to take home to mother, and so on. In the present, he said, the pattern is monogamous dating. The college newspaper reported the article as a perfectly straight reportorial job. At the end of the reportorial account of the article, the writer made the observation that the college president was currently visiting in Europe with one of his wives.

When the young are monogamous in their dating pattern, they are serious; they have some values that they are trying to create out of the muck of society's general values on sex and sexuality. Sometimes I admire what they are trying to create. Often I am infuriated. But just as often this impatience is accompanied by admiration.

The Daily Dartmouth reviewed the movie *The Loved One* (which I haven't seen). Apparently *The Loved One* is full of sexuality badly expressed, a gourmet turned to gluttony. The review was irate in tone. The student writer said, in effect, that we are being "grossed out." That is to say, what is portrayed here is too gross for us to associate with. We refuse to have anything to do with it. Now, the young are able to see the gross in American values and to reject it. They need to be encouraged to do this. They are not automatically going to do it. I am not saying we should leave them to their own devices and they'll be just fine. Not at all. They need to be encouraged and they need to have *your example* and *your explicit encouragement of their moral courage* before they are always willing to do this, but they will do it.

Second admonition: As we try to present sex education in a context which has something implicit, if not explicit, to say about values, we have to have an appreciation of the antic quality of sex, or we are bound to come out wrong in this. We will get overclinical, or overreligious—which is as bad—or overserious, unless we can retain some sense of humor.

Every once in a while I look out of my office window, which sweeps the green, and see a pack of dogs out in the middle of the green, one of them in heat, and the others all milling around with tails wagging. As the pack swirls from one end of the green to the other, the boys walk by laughing. Now that wouldn't go down in any prep school. The headmaster would feel an obligation to be out there with the fire extinguisher, breaking up the assembly! Maybe the boys are right. The antic quality of all these poor, hopeless male dogs suggests something which we dare not lose sight of. We dare not lose sight of it if we mean to be communicative to the young, who *do* appreciate frequently some of the antic qualities in sexuality—in their own sexuality. I don't mean simply explicit sexual activity but the fact of being male and the fact of being female. Every once in a while if you poke a hole in the pretensions of the young, at the right place and in the right way, they will see how ridiculous they look when they are trying to be extremely masculine or extremely feminine.

My twelve-year-old daughter told me after a wonderful lecture on sex in her school, "You know, Daddy, some of the girls went out swinging their hips!" She saw the whole story, the ridiculousness of it, the rightness of it, the whole works.

The third and most serious admonition: *Take a stand.* Set some standards. They may be wrong. The young may prove you're wrong. You may be embarrassed later. You may have to change your mind. Take a stand anyway. The young need you to do that. They need you to kick against. They need you to stand firm for what you believe about sexuality and about sexual behavior. As I say, you may be wrong. That's less important to them than the fact that you are a human being and a person with some courage. If you fear playing God, don't worry. They don't believe you are! You can take a stand for what you think are proper behavioral standards. As I have already mentioned the only rule in the Dartmouth College handbook is: "Gentlemanly conduct is required at all times. Lewdness and fornication are considered a violation of college standards." That produces more conversation between the dean and the student body than any other single issue. A student has never been thrown out of our college for fornication. And I warrant that's not because we have never had fornication. The dean keeps pointing out. "You know, we have never thrown anybody out for this, because the case has never come up." And, in fact, it hasn't. We have thrown people out for lewdness. Students have been expelled for other kinds of misbehavior, but never for fornication. Nevertheless, I think it's important that the college handbook says (whether rightly or wrongly is less important to me), "Fornication is a violation of college standards." The institution must have a public position so that the students will know what the limits are. I am not saying that one should adopt an inflexible posture on these matters. How many of us would be willing to say that sexual intercourse before marriage is normally acceptable, and approvable? How many of us would be willing to say the opposite: that sexual intercourse before marriage is an unforgivable sin?

I am not willing to say that either one of these formulations is correct; and I don't want to say either one of them in an inflexible way. The posture that I think we are required to take is one that says: "There are values in sexual behavior, and they are values that correspond with the following larger human values. . . ." Then we need to discuss the larger human values and back up what we have to say with some humane enforcement that may be available to us through the normal disciplinary arrangements of an educational community, which should strike a balance between respecting the privacy and independence of students and punishing the abuse of persons by each other.

Educators have been characteristically punitive with regard to sexual behavior—or misbehavior, I should say. We are now in the opposite position of being afraid to be punitive at all for fear we will come out looking like Puritans. We are now more commonly afraid to take a stand for what we simply believe: that normally it is not a good thing for people to have premarital intercourse. It may be all right under certain circumstances, with certain persons. It may be both forgivable and good under certain circumstances. But we are not willing to say—most of us— that this is acceptable and is to be encouraged. If we are not willing to say it, we've got to take the same kind of stand on this as we do on matters of intellectual honesty and other things that concern us as educators.

A final admonition: the *real* value crisis we are experiencing is one of *purpose* crisis rather than *value*. We worry about the sexual behavior and the attitude of the young. I worry much more about problems of identity, normlessness, purposelessness. I worry much more about those because they have something to do with the desperate attempt young people sometimes make to find identity through sexual activity. I think this is endemic in the society. We are trying to find our identity through sexual activity, and we are not succeeding. This is partly because we don't have a larger purpose in the service of which our sexual identity can exist.

Let me just conclude by mentioning some moral principles which I think provide a framework within which sexual education can be discussed.

1. Anomie—purposelessness, normlessness—is immoral.
2. Reconciliation is a prime human purpose. We care about harmony among people. We are hurt by division among people. Sexuality discussed in that framework can make a lot of sense.
3. To be human is to be free. And the consequence of being free is to be responsible.
4. Sex is social, not private.
5. Persons are more important than principles.

With those five dicta in mind, I think we can have a framework within which discussion of sexuality, sexual behavior, sexual identity can make a good deal of sense with the young. I think these are things that they understand and believe in inherently.

REV. UNSWORTH'S QUESTION PERIOD

QUESTION: *When you say purposelessness and normlessness are immoral, do you mean immoral in a religious sense?*

REV. UNSWORTH: Well, I don't know any other sense for morality than one that has something to do with religion. I don't mean in *our* religious sense, in a doctrinaire religious sense.

Now, if I could point to the framework for the whole, I

would point to the notion of *freedom within boundaries.* That is, I think, the framework within which sex education, and values concerning sexuality, have to be discussed.

QUESTION: *Why do you say sex is social, not private, rather than social as well as private?*

REV. UNSWORTH: Perhaps *individual* is the more proper word. I get the argument from college students that nobody has a right to make any statements about standards in this area, because this is an area like conscience—totally private—meaning totally individually bound. Sex seems to me the most social of activities, because it is relational and because it has larger social consequences, both in the formation of permanent personality (or the destruction of personality) and the creation of life.

COMMENT: James Pike's book *Teenagers and Sex* develops from a moral point of view the absolute, the way sex has customarily been approached: adults said no premarital sex, no homosexuality—all these were wrong, period. That's all that was ever said. He advocates a new approach, rather like what you are talking about. He has a good chapter on how this can come across to a fifth grader.

COMMENT: I admire that book. Bishop Pike goes on to touch upon moral aspects. He says the objective really ought to be to get boys and girls to be sexually responsible, and not to be so concerned about whether they have premarital relations or whether they marry if there is a pregnancy outside of wedlock. But the question *should* be: "Are you doing something that is right for you and for the other person?"

REV. UNSWORTH: That is the important question, much more important than the technical question about the style of sexual activity. Much has been said earlier by Dr. Calderone and Dr. Guttmacher about technical virginity and about the tendency of society to allow anything just as long as that bridge was not crossed. But now, that doesn't mean to me that you say: "Okay, no more toll gate!" On the contrary. What it means to me is that you say: "Now, sexual relationship exists along a continuum, from holding hands to coitus. Along that continuum there is a corresponding continuum of serious, mature relationship of the total person. There is an appropriateness which follows along. Certain gestures are appropriate to certain degrees of commitment to the other person. What is really immoral, from a religious or simply a rational point of view, is the inappropriateness of a gesture that does not *mean* anything or does not mean what it should inherently mean.

COMMENT: Another point Bishop Pike makes is that you must stress to the students that they reach a stage in their emotional involvement in the preliminaries of sex that may cause them to lose control and not be able to make clear judgments. They need to avoid getting themselves into a position where their values become clouded and they can't think clearly.

COMMENT: I heard recently in a university series on sex education that the real immorality of any sexual relationship is in the exploitation of one partner by the other, and, more specifically, of women by men. Now, in those terms, I understand immorality to be if a man is taking advantage of a woman under false pretenses, or perhaps vice versa, in some situations. That's *real* immorality. Now, if the sexual relationship is enjoyed for its own sake, even though both partners realize that this is very superficial, and it is strictly for sensual pleasure, that, in fact, is a legitimate moral bind.

REV. UNSWORTH: It's a moral bind, all right, but I am not so sure about the legitimacy.

COMMENT: That's the question I wonder if you'd be willing to comment on.

REV. UNSWORTH: Erich Fromm's quote, "You scratch my back, I'll scratch yours. Let's use each other."

COMMENT: Exactly.

REV. UNSWORTH: That is exploitative in the same way. We have all met people who have exploited their own talents. A person with a slick personality can sell ice boxes to the Eskimos. The problem with him is, he does—and he makes a lot of money at it. A college boy I know earned $1,500 one summer, selling encyclopedias to poor people at $15 a crack. They couldn't afford it and he knew they couldn't afford it. After he had made $1,500 this way he was sickened by what he was doing, and quit. He didn't give the $1,500 away or return it or go back and take back the encyclopedias. But at least he quit. At least he was nauseated by what he was doing.

Now, this is an exploitation of a talent. One can exploit his own talents to his own gratification in sex as well as in other ways. The fact that two people decide that they are going to have fun together for the sake of the fun, and disregard the question of relationship implicit in sexual behavior between male and female, seems to me simply exploitative. The fact that they both consent doesn't make it any the less so.

QUESTION: *How do you know when it's exploitation unless you have some governing considerations which might be called principles?*

REV. UNSWORTH: I don't think I denied that principles had to do with this. I would only deny that it is an inflexible principle that one should not have intercourse outside marriage.

COMMENT: All right. You will find those who say that's the *only* principle in thinking about sex education. I'd say that that doesn't help much.

REV. UNSWORTH: There are affirmative rather than negative principles, which underlie what we are saying about exploitation, principles of affirmation of human value and human relationship. You cannot use a person as a thing. That is the principle.

COMMENT: What you said was, "Persons are more important than principles."

REV. UNSWORTH: Yes. That doesn't mean there aren't principles. That just means persons are more important than them. I am wary about allowing talk of principles to take too free a place in this kind of a discussion, because principles frequently turn into legalities. I am afraid of legalism because it's a blind alley in discussing the dynamics of human relationships. Law is the codification of relationships. It is not their liberation. We are talking about the liberation of the human relationship, not its codification.

QUESTION: *Do you liberate into chaos, or into what?*

REV. UNSWORTH: "Freedom within boundaries."

QUESTION: *And boundaries are established by . . . ?*

REV. UNSWORTH: By you.

QUESTION: *Persons, not principles?*

REV. UNSWORTH: Yes. Finally, that's right. That is to say, am I going to reach for an eternal principle to which you must be obedient? The answer is no. The principles of sexual behavior, for example, about which we have been talking here, are principles that are different from those which pertain in the primitive societies that gave rise to the Bible, or that pertain in most primitive societies now, or that pertained in the time of Calvin's Geneva, when the punishment for adultery was execution.

QUESTION: *Are there distinctions between male and female behavior? There has been a fair amount of talk about what it is to be a woman, and what it is to be a man, and they are different. Does this imply that sexual behavior may have a different effect upon a woman than upon a man?*

DR. GUTTMACHER: I would certainly think so. Certainly *anatomically* the man has a distinct difference. And, if a relationship should result in pregnancy, it makes a remarkable difference! The general attitude that you read in the literature is that the sex relation is much more meaningfully experienced by the female, that she is much more deeply involved in it than the male. I think that this sort of thing is written by men. I am not sure they know. I am not certain one can measure the *emotional* impact, but certainly the *physical* difference is great.

As we have heard, college students still have not deserted the double standard to some extent. So not only is there an anatomical difference between men and women, there is a difference in peer regard. Whether there is a difference in emotional reaction—it's hard to find evidence one way or the other.

REV. UNSWORTH: From the point of view of an ethical regard for sexual behavior, there is no difference. Anatomically, yes; psychologically, perhaps; ethically, no. The point here is not that women ought to have greater freedom but that men ought to have greater responsibility. My emphasis would be on the responsibility of the male.

In the development of Western culture, as the female emerges from chattel slavery to equal status as a human being, the degrees of responsibility shared by men and women have tended to level up to each other. There is still a remnant of the double standard. I venture it's far less widely accepted now—even among men, at least of the college generation—than it would have been twenty or thirty years ago.

DR. GUTTMACHER: I would certainly think so.

COMMENT: A study at Vassar indicated that the majority of the girls there did not wish to have intercourse except with the man they were going to marry, either before or after marriage —but a fair percentage of them wished their *mate* to have had experience. That's a curious reverse application of the double standard.

I would like to go back to your points, "to be free is to be responsible," and "persons are more important than principles." I think you ought to develop the psychological and moral attributes that you think of a person as having in this society.

REV. UNSWORTH: When I use the "person" in a context of ethical discussion, I mean a human being endowed with freedom, with inviolable integrity, with creative capacity, and with the desire for self-expression. Each of those, as an aspect of the human being, forms a kind of boundary line upon which no other person has the right to encroach. Anyone may be admitted, invited within those boundaries. Another may be invited into my desire for self-expression. I may consort with another in self-expression intellectually, artistically, sexually, and so on. I may share my integrity with another person on a matter of social moment of some sort. I may stand alongside of that person in a race crisis or in a matter of justice in the courts, and share my integrity. But in all these situations I preserve the right not to be encroached upon, and I must accord to every other person the right not to be encroached upon in those attributes.

Now, that's a very imperfect and partial notion. By *person* I don't mean just another human being, I mean all of these things as an aura.

QUESTION: *If all the boys in college had a really good course in sex education before they came, what influence would that have on your counseling job? Would that make it any easier or any different?*

REV. UNSWORTH: It would make it a whale of a lot easier, I can tell you that.

QUESTION: *In what way?*

REV. UNSWORTH: Well, there was a boy in my office the other day who wouldn't have been there if he'd had that "really good course in sex education." He would have had the sense to use a contraceptive device in spite of the pleading of the juvenile who persuaded him not to, who is now pregnant, whom he is now fighting about marrying, whom he shouldn't marry, for her sake and his and the baby's. The whole psychological, legal, spiritual turmoil that has erupted around him wouldn't have happened. Now, I picked that one not because I approve of his behavior with a sixteen-year-old girl—which probably *also* wouldn't have happened, incidentally, if he had been really mature sexually, himself—he wouldn't have needed a sixteen-year-old partner—but presuming that he *did* get involved in a sexual relationship, he at least would have had sense enough to know his responsibility to avoid a pregnancy. This would have made a lot of difference.

A great deal of the counseling and the public problems that I see and have to deal with are related to latent homosexuality in young men of college age. They are uncertain about their sexual identity. In panic at this uncertainty, they do all sorts of ridiculous things which cause all sorts of trouble. They could be set at ease about a lot of this. I think of that case which Dr. Calderone mentioned—the student who came back to school after having had a homosexual advance made to him, terrified that he must actually be a homosexual because somehow he attracted a homosexual advance. The widespread fear of latent homosexuality in college-age men is just amazing. We would be spared a great deal if they were liberated from that fear or were prepared at least to cope with it. I suppose everybody has to cope with it.

QUESTION: *There is an enormous area of education which is in the hands of the religious institutions, called religious education. To what extent do you think the formal religious institutions have a responsibility to include in this field of religious education the area of sexual morality? To what extent is this possible?*

REV. UNSWORTH: Obviously, to me, they have an overriding responsibility here. They must not pretend to be the biologists, and the medical people, and the psychiatrists, but if the religious institution can't say something significant about the redemptive capacity of human relationship, who can?

QUESTION: *Are they doing this? And if they are not doing this, is it possible that they can?*

REV. UNSWORTH: Well, number one, they aren't doing it effectively enough. Number two, yes, there is a possibility they can. Number three, some of them are. The people involved in religious education who write the materials do a better job than does the Sunday school teacher into whose hands this material falls. In general, the *curriculum material* as provided by the main churches is pretty good. At least, it's not as inadequate as the caricature we might be tempted to draw. But *what actually happens* can be criminal. I was asked to talk to the adult Sunday school class of a church about sex ethics. As part of the series the class was reading a book by Roger Shinn, and one of the chapters had to do with this. I was to discuss this chapter. I didn't know it, but the high school students had been invited to sit in on this session. So I had high school children and parents. Now, what do you do in that situation? I am not sure what you do, but I was determined that I was not going to give a lecture. So, I said: "How many parents think there is any consensus on what the church ought to teach its young about sex?" A lot of hands went up. Then I started asking questions about what the consensus was, and the hands went down! We couldn't get agreement among the parents about what the values were. (Incidentally, I had insisted that the youngsters sit separately from each other so that they wouldn't get together and titter.) I asked them, "Right now, this is your chance. You tell them what you think the church ought to be teaching you." There was a heavy silence. They were afraid to mention the subject. So, we started to talk about sex in explicit detail. There were nods of agreement from the teen-agers, but little articulation. I finally said: "Now, look, the teen-agers are not being fair to their parents. Before I say another word, I've got to have *one* teen-ager who is going to tell me what he thinks the church has been saying. Regardless of whether he thinks it's the right or wrong thing to say, tell me what you think the church has been saying." There was a long silence, and finally one young tenth-grade boy said, "Well, I think they've been saying sex is wrong, sort of in general, but I don't know why." And on that note our time ran out, and we dismissed the class.

I don't know that much progress has been made, but at least

the agenda is now prepared among the teen-agers and the adults in that one group.

If you are asking about the church as an institution, the answer can be a fairly affirmative one. If you ask about the church as a group of human beings with all sorts of inadequacies and problems to overcome as parents, as citizens, and as sexual human beings themselves, the answer doesn't come out quite so well.

QUESTION: *Do I understand you to say that premarital sex experience can be either immoral or moral?*

REV. UNSWORTH: Yes, I think I would stand by that.

QUESTION: *You know, this makes it real tough, doesn't it? Where are your guidelines, your principles that we are going to give them?*

REV. UNSWORTH: Well, I go back to the question I raised earlier. "How many think it should be the normal thing for youngsters of seventeen, eighteen, nineteen years of age, before marriage, to experience sexual intercourse with one or more persons as a more or less regular affair?" We don't get a whole lot of takers for that. I think our lack of enthusiasm for that statement suggests what our norm really is. That doesn't mean, however, that sexual intercourse before marriage is automatically, under all circumstances, irretrievably immoral, does it? That doesn't leave us without guidelines. It leaves us with room for meeting human persons in human situations, with all the variations of those.

QUESTION: *Just for kicks, why not? Why* isn't *it bad? Why* isn't *it immoral? Why isn't it always wrong? Isn't that silly?*

REV. UNSWORTH: What, the question?

COMMENT: Yes.

REV. UNSWORTH: No. That's the question most people are afraid to ask, because they *think* it's silly.

COMMENT: Thank you for helping me!

REV. UNSWORTH: Well, I can conceive, and I am sure you can, of a relationship between two young people which is barred from becoming a marriage relationship by some irrational factor which should not get in their way, and which they have to wait out. They may decide to establish what in English tradition we call common-law marriage. They may decide that they are going to have intercourse with each other because they intend a permanent relationship of serious consequence for themselves. But they are not permitted the privilege of marriage, for economic reasons, because of parental objection, or the law, if it's an interracial marriage in certain states, and so on. There may be any number of irrational, unjustifiable barriers to the marriage. If they happened to be Negro and white in Virginia, they had to wait until they could get out of the state or until the Supreme Court overturned that law. Pick whatever irrational barrier you want. Now, I can imagine lots of set situations in which I would have to say that a sexual relationship is a moral affirmation, a moral relationship, would you not?

COMMENT: Yes, I would.

COMMENT: That isn't good enough, because you've hung your example on a negative, rather than finding a positive—the negative being the law in Virginia, for instance.

REV. UNSWORTH: All right. Let me put it in another way. If we can talk in terms of norms and exceptions, one can imagine an exception to almost any serious norm, which exception nevertheless comports with the norm, no?

COMMENT: All right.

REV. UNSWORTH: The exception can be on an affirmative or negative basis. It can be prompted affirmatively or negatively. Isn't that so?

COMMENT: Yes.

REV. UNSWORTH: Take stealing, for example. The norm is "Don't steal." One can think of lots of examples where a person *should* steal, affirmatively should steal, in order to meet a positive human value. That doesn't make stealing right. That means that under this set of circumstances the norm permits an exception in the name of the respective persons, in the name of affirmation of human life.

COMMENT: *Les Misérables.*

REV. UNSWORTH: Yes.

COMMENT: I don't see why you still can't say that the principle is: *Don't steal.*

REV. UNSWORTH: Well, you can. And most of us do.

COMMENT: But you don't when it comes to sex.

REV. UNSWORTH: I am uncomfortable with the language of principle, because we have equated principles with *absolute* principles. That's usually what we mean by principles; absolutes, perfectly inflexible. Principle has become for us not norm but legality in our common language. That's why I am skittish about the word *principle*. If you want to use the word *principle* the way I am using the word *norm,* fine.

QUESTION: *When you say normal standards, normal standards for whom? I can see where you would have one set of norms for the students going to the schools represented here. I can think of another set of norms represented by the people in* Manchild in the Promised Land. *Are you willing to comment on the moral aspects of these different norms?*

REV. UNSWORTH: Yes, I am willing to try. Is it immoral for a woman living in a Negro ghetto to say, "I want a child, but I don't want a man?" Is it possible for her to say that morally —for that to be a moral affirmation and aspiration?

DR. GUTTMACHER: That's not wholly moral, because she is not thinking through the consequences to the child. I am not sure that that's moral.

QUESTION: *According to* her *standards, though, directed within herself to that point where she is presently educated?*

DR. GUTTMACHER: She is merely exploiting the child under these conditions.

REV. UNSWORTH: Well, is she?

COMMENT: Not necessarily.

REV. UNSWORTH: What are the consequences to the child?

DR. GUTTMACHER: I think the consequence to the child of being raised in poverty is bad enough. Being raised *illegitimately* in poverty is certainly a heck of a stone around your neck.

COMMENT: I don't think it would be such a stigma in a Negro ghetto, fortunately, or unfortunately. I think the question of being raised without a father might be more important.

DR. GUTTMACHER: That's what I was thinking.

REV. UNSWORTH: Given the possibility of the child's being raised without a father in marriage or being raised without a father *out of* marriage, which is the choice that often faces the test-case woman we are talking about, is it then a moral possibility for her to aspire to have a child, to have a family, without having a man? I think it is, myself. I may be short-sighted about this. I think that it's quite conceivable for that to be a moral affirmation, a moral desire, even though it has certain immoral possibilities in it prompted by the sickness and immorality in society that creates this situation for her.

Human mastery over physical life has extended widely in recent decades. With the extension of mastery goes the extension of responsibility in fearsome degree. I've just been sitting in on a medical student seminar discussing death and dying. Immediately when you talk about death and dying to medical students, you talk about mastery over the process of life, and about what is the ethical responsibility to insert the tube for intravenous feeding, or to withdraw the tube. Either way, you are exercising mastery. There is no avoiding this mastery. The Hippocratic oath has a modern flaw in it. We are supposed to preserve life. Now we can preserve life in unconscionable and unjustifiable degree. So with that mastery goes an extension of responsibility, and a nakedness of responsibility, when a man stands in front of the capacity to administer life or death.

Now similar mastery is present in sexual intercourse, in the whole range of sexual activity. And with that mastery goes the absolute, raw, unprotected necessity of taking on yourself the responsible decision. The question is cast differently from the way it has ever been cast before in human history.

SIXTH SESSION:
OPEN DISCUSSION BY
THE AUDIENCE

NATHANIEL FRENCH, CHAIRMAN: What is the program that should be instituted in our schools? What ought the program in sex education to be? And what can we of the National Association of Independent Schools do about it across the country?

COMMENT: I think the problems of the secondary schools are very much like the colleges' problems ten years ago. At that time we heard a sigh of relief because we were told that young people wouldn't ask about contraceptives until they went to college. Everything has moved down to a younger age, and we certainly ought to take this into consideration.

COMMENT: Two years ago some of our eighth graders told a teacher they were disturbed by the numbers of boys in the eighth grade who were using Saran Wrap as a contraceptive. The school doctor told me that this has become a national problem. There is even a medical term for some of the irritations which occur this way. Certainly in the wealthy suburbs you can't wait for seventeen.

COMMENT: Any suggestions we make must be for schools that receive children at ninth-grade level and younger. One kind of program will be appropriate for schools which cover the entire elementary and secondary years and another for those that are elementary only or secondary only.

COMMENT: In the same way we learn mathematical facts or spelling rules we must learn the biological facts, right at the start. Perhaps the fifth grade would be a good time to introduce a course or fruitful discussion with boys and girls about the reproduction system. Any of us who have dealt with this at that age find it is much easier to handle than we used to think it would be. It is not loaded with the overtones that adults sometimes inadvertently give it. And certainly the committee should recommend at least a course on reproduction in the early grades of the elementary school. That's one.

COMMENT: Since our school starts with four-year-olds, I would not begin with a course in reproduction. But children of this age ask questions about sex. The way they are answered is extremely important. So I would suggest that we begin with advice for parents and teachers in how to answer the questions of young children. This would help answer the questions in the right way. And it would give the school a good contact with parents from the beginning. If we work parents and faculty together from the beginning, it will be better than having either parents or teachers try to do it alone.

COMMENT: In our elementary school we have bright young ladies who stay three, four, and maybe five years and then leave to marry and raise a family. Whatever the classroom programs in sex education are, schools need a person of some stability on the faculty who is in charge of the school-wide program.

COMMENT: With four- and five-year-olds, I think it should be the person who is closest to them, whether it's their parents or their classroom teacher who deals with these special questions, and certainly not someone who just comes in for the occasion.

DR. GUTTMACHER: I think we are talking about two different things. One is the inborn sex education that intelligent people give in their contact with children. This is magnificent, and essential. The advantage of having some type of formalized structure for the knowledge, perhaps in the fifth grade, is obvious. It brings the thing together. And it brings the *group* together. Students see this as a group activity rather than a personal activity involving only individual and teacher. It's healthy for the children within the group to exchange ideas, to see each other ask questions and to have the interplay that a group situation gives. You obviously begin as soon as the child enters school, but that is a very different type of teaching from what I am talking about for the fifth grade.

COMMENT: When we were a smaller school, we had a man who taught science all through the school, upper and lower. He became the center of the effort on sex education and it was eminently successful. It was successful because of what he *was,* not because of the nature of the program. But it did serve to hold the program together too, and to make sure that it did get carried out.

COMMENT: With us, it happens to be the nurse, but it doesn't matter who it is as long as it's done consistently.

COMMENT: In the fall of the year, we ask all of the parents of children in our pre-first grade to come with the teachers to meet with a medical doctor and a psychiatrist for a series of sessions, one night a week for six weeks. This way we get all the parents of the incoming children well indoctrinated. We do not try to repeat this for the first, second, and third grades, because those are the same parents, but we do ask our teachers of these grades always to come in. Consequently, we have a constant review of information and interest for teachers.

COMMENT: I'd like to suggest that we concentrate our efforts on a program from kindergarten through high school, and then let each independent school adapt it to its own people, style, and curriculum. Many of us are concerned about who in our own schools should handle the program. Maybe some type of a summer program or workshop can be set up for the training of representatives from our various schools. We might get together a list of the materials and literature available, and have that at the workshop, in hopes that they would take this back to their home schools and try to institute a program.

CHAIRMAN: Dr. Guttmacher, Mrs. McIntosh said that the Brearley

School had a pretty good collection of animals for the children to watch and play with. Then they began at the sixth grade to talk about having babies. There seemed to be no carry-over from the earlier experience at all. I wonder if the greatest difficulty isn't the problem of the special urges and confusions which the *adolescent* student feels that the elementary student does not.

DR. GUTTMACHER: You've got to bring the thing down to *humans.* The child is not satisfied with a comparative anatomy study in zoology between humans and animals. After all he's interested in his own species. I kept three or four human embryos in various stages of development to show the children the growth of the fetus. This was most exciting for the children to see, the fetus at eight, fifteen, and twenty-six weeks.

I've tried to teach reproductive physiology as a kind of laboratory course, by dissecting animals, showing the spermatozoa of the rat—that's all fine. But you've got to bring the focus down to what we are talking about, the human being himself. If you remain with bees and butterflies—or rats—you cannot make the point. That was fine forty years ago but we've gone far beyond that. Probably 75 percent of our concentration should be on humans and 25 percent on comparative studies.

COMMENT: Most of our secondary school students know the biological facts. They might have some facts confused but this is easy to clarify. Dealing with their own emotions and attitudes is the most difficult thing for us. My interest would be in concentrating on what to do with your sexuality, once you understand the biological facts.

COMMENT: Considering the hundreds of years of Sunday school teaching and church preaching, I am not so sure that the frontal attack on attitudes and values is the most effective. By the attention we would devote to the factual aspects of sex we would be beginning to create in the young person's mind an understanding of the magnitude of this whole process. Through this attention would come, for many, an appreciation of the magic and mystery of it all, and also an attitude toward sex which is beyond the purely factual. You cannot regard sex as purely a mechanistic process, once you begin to understand the intricacies of it. It seems to me that this would be an inevitable by-product of our study.

REV. UNSWORTH: The frontal attack is the only one that saves the soup sometimes. By frontal attack, I mean a direct facing of the question. I do not mean an aggressive approach.

COMMENT: I had reference largely to young children, say, ten-year-olds. You can address yourself directly to the older ones. But if there is an undergirding of factual information, and attention given to this in a positive way, so that the information isn't being acquired around the corner and behind the door, you are going to create a climate in which there is a better attitude toward sex.

The climate is perhaps the key to the whole thing. If it starts early enough, you will have youngsters coming into adolescence with a much better attitude. To ten-year-olds you can start talking a little bit more directly about values, about the kind of relationship that Mother and Father have. Dr. Calderone mentioned that children often have an antiseptic, unemotional view of sex. They think every once in a while parents who otherwise have no sexual contact decide it's time to have a baby, and the whole process works like a hypodermic! You make this clinical decision, go through this ritual, and up comes a baby. Now, by ten or eleven years old, children already appreciate in a vivid way the sexual dimension of the relationship between their parents. And if intercourse has become a biological factor in their comprehension by eleven years old, let's say, then it ought to be discussed with a full sense of propriety and delicacy with regard to their feelings. It ought not to be hidden that their mother and father go through this ritual of consummation themselves.

COMMENT: That's part of the factual information that should be shared, that the act of intercourse is one of pleasure which is indulged in frequently by people who are married and some who are not, and that the act of procreation is an occasional aspect of the sexual act.

REV. UNSWORTH: When we are talking about that sort of thing with eleven-year-olds, we are talking about values. We are trying to create an atmosphere in which the fact exists. The atmosphere is charged with value assumptions.

COMMENT: I suppose, then, I really did mean by a frontal attack *a didactic approach.* This is what we must shy away from.

REV. UNSWORTH: I'd prefer to shy away from that with people of any age.

QUESTION: *What is the impact on children when one of those questions come up that nobody has an answer to? If you say, "I don't know," or "I don't know what I think," are you inadvertently teaching what might be considered undue permissiveness?*

QUESTION: *How about the question, "Are you in favor of premarital intercourse?"*

COMMENT: A very healthy technique that works in our home is the teen-age bull session. Let them talk it out. You really get into values. I don't know if this is possible in a school but in our home it's the greatest. The children invite their friends in, boys and girls.

QUESTION: *But you are present?*

COMMENT: Yes—and my wife.

COMMENT: A lot of parents would feel unwelcome in a situation like that.

COMMENT: They invite us in and then they kick us out. It's just an open bull session. Anything goes.

COMMENT: The difference between that kind of situation and a school is apparent. You are a *parent* speaking to them, or, as you suggest, mostly listening to them. It's all under the auspices of an individual, whereas if you do it in the classroom, it's under the auspices of the institution.

QUESTION: *Well, you still come to the question: What do you say if they ask you, "Are you in favor of premarital intercourse?"*

COMMENT: I tell them what I believe. They tear it apart. They don't agree with it at all. In fact, they are much more conservative than I am.

QUESTION: *You must be a lot surer about some of these questions than a lot of us around this table. That's the part that bothers me. A teacher is suddenly faced in the classroom with a question that he is uncertain about. Where does he go from there?*

COMMENT: I think any teacher who is uncertain about a question had better duck it.

COMMENT: I don't agree. To the question that hits one of us on which he has a conviction, I think he could stand up and say: "I personally believe this." He can do this in the classroom as well as someone else can do it in the home. I think what hangs us up here is when we suddenly see ourselves *not* as individuals but as teachers, as administrators. We feel suddenly called upon to have an answer that's universally applicable.

COMMENT: And there isn't one.

COMMENT: There isn't one. We can say that we personally don't know of an answer to a certain question and we don't happen to know of anybody who has one, but we can say what we personally believe.

COMMENT: As we talk about questions we prove that we are more insecure than the children. We have talked so many times here of what is right and what is wrong. Or we've talked about what immorality is. There are probably as many different feelings about morality as there are different people in the room. The issue is not what any one of us in this room thinks. It is instead that each child that asks these questions is searching for some guidelines to use in making decisions on his own. Our job is more counseling than teaching. If we direct the question back to the student, "What do you think?"—well, he *will* think something or he would not have brought the question up in the first place. With the right kind of questions, he will draw his own conclusions as to what is right and what is wrong. His own conclusions, in all probability, will be as good as our conclusions. We are all confronted throughout our own lives with these very same decisions ourselves.

COMMENT: What happens *after* we answer by saying, "What do *you* think?" In the *Look* article, the boys asked Dr. Calderone, "What do you think about premarital intercourse?" And she answered, "What do you think?" I looked at this and I thought this really sounded like the way to evade the issue or play coy. But by the time she was finished with that extraordinary session a rather impressive series of things had gone after the student's "What do *you* think?" She brought these students out —exactly where she thought they ought to come out, because she felt she had more to offer on this than they had. In other words, she guided, challenged, and inspired them *after* turning the "What do you think?" back on them.

REV. UNSWORTH: Here we are back with The Big Question of are you for or against premarital intercourse. It would appear that the framework of our sense of what is moral is an absolute and legalistic thing, a framework conditioned by our feeling that we must necessarily control the morality of the young. If we say "Yes," we are controlling their sexual activity by precipitating them into it. If we say "No," we are holding a standard that we know to be not universally applicable, although we may be doing them some good. That is not how the young think morally, or how any of us do. They think in terms of what is normal and what is exceptional, and that's the way we think. We have far too little faith in their ability to sort out these things. If we say "No," they can easily write that off and go their merry way if they wish. If we say "Under certain circumstances," they are perfectly ready and willing to say, "I'm a human being. I have to decide what the circumstances are. I am not going to let my teacher decide it for me." The two things I'd like to keep in view are these: (1) A sense of candor about the way we think morally, which we can afford to share with the young. (2) A sense of responsible guidelines which we owe them.

A youngster also says, "May I have permission to do so and so?" He is really asking for a negative response but not actually willing to ask: "Will you please tell me *not* to do the following?" We have to be smart enough to see that sometimes what's being requested is "No." Normal guidelines are fairly accessible to us. I asked earlier, "Who believes that under normal circumstances it ought to be normal dating experience for seventeen-year-olds to have sexual intercourse prior to marriage?" Nobody seemed to believe that. So what are we saying? We are saying: "Normally, this is bad. It has risks. It has psychological risks, as well as physical risks. It has social risks that are far too important, far too heavy to be borne in the name of experimentation, pleasure, or any of the other usual rationalizations. Therefore, don't get mixed up in this kind of thing. If you want to know an answer, there's an answer." They have to take this and use it as they will. I don't think this is as complex, difficult, obscure, or inaccessible as we think it is.

CHAIRMAN: Part of this is going to be complex and obscure for a lot of schoolmasters, however, and I am one of them. I agree that you have to be frank. And I agree that the notion of the norm and the exceptional is a sensible and workable one. How is my daughter going to know, as a freshman in college, with all those wolves of Fraternity X, what's normal? They are *all* going to tell her what's normal.

REV. UNSWORTH: You have really done your job. There was a theologian on the Stanford campus, now dead, Alexander Miller. In his book *The Man in the Mirror,* he deals with ethics in a case study approach. He talks about the young girl who comes to discuss this question. The pressure is on from the fraternity boy she goes with and from the context which the fraternity provides for them. She says, "Now, what am I supposed to do?" And he says, "What is your reference? Why are you hesitant about going ahead?" She says, "You know, when I come right down to it, the only thing that I can think of is that my mother told me it was a bad idea. I would feel disloyal to my mother if I went ahead with this."

Miller said, "What's the matter with that? That's a fine, upstanding moral principle. That's as good a basis for a moral decision as you'll ever have: 'Mother told me so.'"

Now, a youngster wants to say: "I've got to have a rational or an absolute religious basis." This is the kind of thing we are searching for, though most of us really believe what we do believe because Mother told us so, somewhere way back when. I think we underestimate the power of parental affirmation. Its carry-over power is enormous.

COMMENT: You don't get in trouble with young ladies like Mr. Miller's. It's when Mother tells her two things in opposite directions that you have difficulty.

COMMENT: I talked this over with twenty seniors in a group and the question is not as open-ended as it appears to be from the way we have been discussing it. The children are asking not about the desirability of premarital sexual activity but rather about the reasons for postponement and restraint. They know —I don't think you have to remind them—they know they are free to act as they wish to act. But in the course of such a discussion you can take up such things as one of the points that Jules Henry makes in his book on American culture. We have a consumer culture now. We have every force trying to break down impulse. On the other hand, you can talk to them aesthetically. You can talk about the values of postponement, so that their sexuality will be more mature, fulfilling sexuality when they finally consummate a relationship. The students talk very frankly and openly about this, and they do *want* to talk about these values.

COMMENT: What do you say about the girl who suddenly appears in your office with this question, and puts it on a clear-cut basis? She went away to college and she was told she was going to have a good time. But on the first date somebody made advances, and she decided she didn't want that. Since she didn't give in, the rumor spread around that she's not the kind of girl that will socialize, so to speak. Since that time, she doesn't get around at all. She asks, "Now what do I do? These are all the things you told me were the right things to do, and now I'm the wallflower." Since so many are having premarital intercourse, isn't it far better that we give out some concrete information? They are going to pick it up anyway, so they may as well have it accurately. We can hope that we are going to have an effect on them and that the lectures and discussions are going to prevent trouble, but in the meantime, just in case we may be wrong, I think we'd better give out that information. We've been wrong about other things. I'd hate to think that we failed them that way too.

COMMENT: I have the uneasy feeling that you are making a very difficult question more difficult than it is, by really sort of feeling consciously or not that you have been bypassed by a revolution. You are afraid that you may have been. Therefore, you are afraid that you are going to fail in the efforts you are going to make. Let me put it the other way round. What you are really asked to do is *to say what you believe* and what you therefore think ought to be done. You may be afraid nobody is going to listen to you. This puts too much certainty on the revolution having bypassed you.

    Actually the image of a revolution is a wrong one in this whole context. Human behavior and societal behavior don't happen in terms of a revolution. The word should really be *change*. Society is constantly in a state of change, and it is not always a change in one direction—it goes back and forth. The changes are brought about by what the established order—the older people, the experienced people—say they believe.

The "revolution" we talk about has happened in other places and at other times. And it's been changed and reversed, it's gone one way, then the other, because of what the experienced, older people—call it the adult power structure—have done.

Now, we are afraid of this for a number of reasons: (1) The number of young people is greater than it was in the past. But, if we accept this as the only rationale, we are abdicating to the domination by the majority. (2) The other one is the economic aspect, or the economic pressures. But all of this does not change the basic question. You are being asked to say what you believe and what you expect. I think you are outguessing too much whether you are going to fail in making an impact. Now, you *may* fail, or you may not, but that's true in any aspect of education. I don't think there is much profit in trying too much to guard yourself against failure, if you do what you think you ought to be doing.

COMMENT: As a Southerner, I begin with an inherent advantage, I think, over people in New England. We have General Lee in front of us and we know that General Lee is perfect, therefore *we* can't be perfect; whereas the people in New England have nobody between them and God! My point is, I think we are all longing to get the answer, so that, when we give this rational answer to a young person, he won't have any opportunity to say, "No, I am not going to do what you want me to do." Now, as I heard Dr. Guttmacher and Dr. Calderone, they talked about sexuality as being really rooted in the creation. And from my point of view, if this is true, it's rooted in the energy dynamics of—I'll say—the living God. It's just *there*.

I think one of the basic assumptions we have to make is that this "revolution" is a tremendous *expansion of freedom*. And all we can do is say: "Here is the wisdom of the human race as we have received it. Now you act upon it." We have not made this assumption. We have been saying: "I've got to have the right answer to give to young people." I think this is one of the greatest sins of all the independent schools.

COMMENT: I think we take away the autonomy of the student somehow when we say: "We are in charge of your life. What we say you will do." When the student is an autonomous person, he has learned in his education that he is responsible for his own life, for his decisions. *He* should judge what he is doing. When he asks us about what we believe, he is searching for one more set of data. We owe it to him to tell him what we believe. This doesn't mean necessarily that he must follow what we tell him. But perhaps he can use this bit of knowledge, with some of the other things that have come to him, before he makes the decisions that he must make. To somehow take away his autonomy and say we are molding him into what we want him to be would be to do the opposite of what we are trying to do as educators.

REV. UNSWORTH: We have all gotten upset at one time or another about the false quality of relationship between the generations which is endemic to American culture, and is best expressed in that cartoon in *The New Yorker* which shows a student sitting with a pile of books and papers in front of him, and his father coming in wearing a tennis sweater and visor cap and carrying a racket, and the student is saying: "Dad, I don't *need* a buddy!" We sense the false note of that relationship between the generations. We are properly concerned about communication between the generations but improperly concerned about *acceptance* by the young. You know, one way you form yourself at any age is by having an enemy. That is why adolescents need older people! I am quite serious about that. They have to have an enemy in order to know themselves. We serve them very badly if we refrain from standing firmly where we are and being irascible so-and-sos, because we don't agree with them. I would say a much more important question for them and for us is: *how do we gain our own personal freedom to be who we are in front of them, no matter how well it goes down?* This is the only way we can really serve them.

COMMENT: There is another related problem: how can we help young people whose own parents are going through a breakup?

This is getting at what's been troubling me. We agreed that in the lower grades you answer questions honestly. At fifth grade you start teaching certain basic facts. Then you skip up to where you teach them about contraception and making their decisions. Well, there is a long time in there where they want to know who they are. They need all kinds of help in understanding themselves. As Mary Calderone says, it's sexuality not just the genital facts that they need to understand. I don't think you can help that. If you follow along through those years, you don't have the troubles at the end.

COMMENT: We want to get across the great broad vision of it all, beginning with age four. We also want to have moments when we can stop and say, *this* we will emphasize here, and *this* we will emphasize there, and this is how we will do it. At the same time, we are all haunted by the last student who asked us some reverberating question, and the next person who will ask us still another reverberating question. We've got to do everything at once, and it's tough. We just can't withdraw and think of the Great Scheme and how if people grow up in the Great Scheme teachers won't even get these reverberating questions fifteen years from now. This may be true, but we are going to get them tomorrow, if not fifteen years from now.

QUESTION: *What about this* in loco parentis *business. How do people here feel about acting* in loco parentis? *Isn't this what we must do? Doesn't this in a sense answer how you deal with the child whose parents are breaking up?*

COMMENT: I wouldn't think that *literally* you act *in loco parentis.* This would be a great mistake. The parents should be brought in, and there should be some kind of a joint understanding arrived at. We are very wrong in acting *in loco parentis,* and not involving the parents more than we are doing. We are trying to carry all of it when we should be carrying it *with* the parents, and not apart from them.

COMMENT: But our parents are two thousand miles away.

COMMENT: Even so, in a crisis, when there is a breakup in the family, they should not be allowed to be two thousand miles away.

COMMENT: I come from a wealthy community where our children are in some ways terribly overprivileged. It's a coeducational school. We do a very good job of starting with the four-year-olds—perhaps that's the most professionally-run portion of our school—and, incidentally, I think the easiest portion to run.

We do a pretty good job of factual presentation somewhere around the fifth or sixth grade, and this is done by experts. But what happens after that? A lot of you are saying that the children in your schools do or should do something which never happens in my school to the extent that it obviously does in yours, that youngsters are exposing themselves thoughtfully, frankly, and constantly in classes—mathematics, English, history—dealing always with their deep, deep problems and concerns of sexuality, etc., etc., etc. Your teachers evidently have the wisdom to open-end the discussions. The children presumably can go away with some of the answers. We still haven't hit upon what happens *after* grade five or six, after the good factual presentation. We need more help than we are confessing on how we go about this.

Another thing: our children don't *talk* to adults. I don't think they are the most unique people in the world, but they don't talk to adults about their problems. Adults are off limits. Or honest talk with them is off limits. It's not done. Or it's done only occasionally by the aggressive, estranged child. Now, we have had to do something which is entirely different. We had to go into the city's university to get college students in the school for social research—and wearing—many of them highly intellectual—tall black boots, tight black pants, leather jackets, and beards. These very bright young people sit down with our students, with no teachers present, and we begin to get some talk and some communication, which eventually filters back to us. What I really want out of this is not a further discussion of that practice, which has helped us somewhat, but to know what procedures ought to be followed in a variety of schools. What procedures should be followed, first, to encourage youngsters to talk? Though certain teachers may get students beyond the seventh-grade level to speak up, most of them don't have the capacity or the time to encourage this talk enough. There's got to be some other mechanism to get at least my isolated group to the point where they expose their problems and their concerns in a more healthy way, so that we can then combat what we know truly exists in their minds.

COMMENT: We are terribly worried about giving answers. We want to serve *in loco parentis*. We want to be able to tell them what to do about the broken family. We want to be educators.

We want to be teachers. Sometimes we want to play God, although we say we don't. We are terribly humble. For some reason, we don't seem to be able *to be ourselves*. We're too humble. We think we have to be an educational entity of some sort. This is why the children find it hard to talk to the adult generation. They are not talking to me as a person, they are talking to a headmistress. And who the hell wants to talk to a headmistress? When they come to me, and say "What do you think?" And when I say, "I, myself, as a person, think thus and so," they have a real, live person they are talking to, and they can agree or disagree with that person. But when I put on my headmistress hat, and say, "Tell me what *you* think," and start playing the operator and trying to get things out of them, then they don't want to talk. I seem to them *not a person.* I am what they call an "unperson" in some places, and they'd rather talk to the beard or the leather jacket. Now, what is the matter with us that we can't be people?

QUESTION: *Is the isolated girl talking to you? Is it a small group or what?*

COMMENT: I don't think it's any accident that they talk to the gentleman who spoke earlier in his living room. They talk to him because he is *not* being the executive director of a foundation when he talks to those kids in his house. He's being himself. He's not even being a parent. He's being a *person,* and they talk to him.

QUESTION: *You aren't just saying that all we should do is reach those who are able to articulate a concern, are you?*

COMMENT: We have to establish communications before we can talk about *anything.* You asked, what do you say to the child with a home that's breaking up? You may never have had your own home breaking up, but each of us has had a lot of problems to deal with in life. Maybe *as a person,* as *you,* you can talk to the girl who is asking for perspective or understanding, and tell her that life is often hard and that all of us have to meet problems.

QUESTION: *But you are still confining this type of healthy association to those who want to talk, to confide, to ask. How do we get at the large group including those who generally need more help than those who are articulating their problems?*

COMMENT: My oldest child is concerned that some of her friends are not able to communicate with their parents about the problems of sex. Someone in the field of child development said that if the young child's first question isn't taken seriously and answered honestly, the child then learns that this question is not something he can ask. This means he cannot ask all those other questions about being a person that mean the road is open to communicating with the adult world. People in day schools are in a particularly fine position to communicate with parents who are not communicating with this large group of children who have learned they can't talk to their parents.

QUESTION: *What do you do when you discover that the children think adults aren't people one can talk to?*

COMMENT: Some sort of a workshop for your parents, with a good child psychiatrist, might uncover a whole lot of problems that the parents are not communicating to anybody.

COMMENT: We have done that and have had parents say, "Oh, we have no problem at home!" When you get the children on the side, the children certainly don't agree with that. They don't feel they can talk to their parents. So the school *has* to do something. The school has to set up some avenue of approach to *all* the children.

COMMENT: Maybe as only a second-year headmistress I haven't been seasoned long enough not to have confidence in my faculty!

COMMENT: I suspect that I am in the tiny minority of unmarried, never-having-been-married, people in this room. And it strikes me that the way in which Dr. Calderone sees this whole question of sexuality makes sense to me as I look at my faculty. It doesn't matter to me whether they are married, single, male, or female, happily married or unhappily married or whatever. They are communicating themselves to the girls every day of the week. You ask, "How do you get the girls to communicate?" The time comes when the child "knows" a certain teacher from a reaction in an academic situation. She begins to predict the teacher's reaction in another situation. The way a widowed history teacher answers questions about history and world affairs, Viet Nam, Latin America, tells the youngster something. When that child has a family problem, or parents who are about to be divorced, she will have the basis in experience with her teachers, to say, *"That's* the person I can go to and say, 'What am I going to do?' " She will identify the teacher whom *she* finds approachable.

But what about the next step. When we *have* been approached. What do we do? It sometimes seems to me that the only question that the girls are really asking in so many different ways is, "Should I have intercourse before marriage?" Yet some are even asking, "Should I marry?" This comes from the girls whose mothers have married, and married, and married!

COMMENT: It's interesting to go into a school where the students never discuss anything beyond impersonal, superficial things with the teachers or with each other. Again and again, I have talked with students in a school who will privately, almost conspiratorially, raise some searching personal question. I'll say, "Where does this kind of thing get discussed around here?" He says, *"Nowhere.* I'd get murdered if I raised something like this with the others." But then there will be a boy I meet a few minutes later who will raise the same kind of question and he says the same thing—doesn't know that there is anybody else in the school that's aware of this kind of thing, that thinks about this kind of thing. The word hasn't gotten around that there are at least *two* people in the school with the same concern. The one thing each is sure of is that people just don't talk about these things in that school. In other schools students seem to be discussing these things all the time, sometimes to the point that they get sick of it, and they say: "Let's shift to baseball, or *anything,* because this is getting just too much!" I suspect that in the schools where these concerns are discussed usefully there are teachers who already have had some effect in freeing the students to do this. And it isn't always just the perceptive teacher of literature or the helpfully frank biology teacher, either. You don't always get the relaxed, living room bull session atmosphere. Yet somehow it happens. If, as school heads, you can identify teachers who have somehow created an easy and "human" atmosphere around them, then *these* are the people to send to the institutes and workshops on sex education. Those teachers may be the ones that carry the ball for you. They are "inside" the curriculum. They aren't hauled in for a lecture series.

COMMENT: I, too, work in one of these affluent suburbs. Oddly enough, we have a very healthy atmosphere about answering questions. Yet I've worried because after, say, ninth grade we don't get large numbers coming in to have questions answered. We work with a few and answer their questions directly. But just three weeks ago we started a program with our seniors, on a voluntary basis, and had a highly skilled psychiatrist come in to talk with any seniors who wanted to have any questions answered one evening each week. This has grown in three weeks so that we have 100 percent attendance of our seniors. We also welcome a few of their friends, at their request.

Now, these seniors are going to help us introduce this kind of experience to the rest of the school. I think one has to be patient in something like this, and just let it grow.

COMMENT: We've got to be patient with these individual or small group conversations until we have built up some kind of pattern or atmosphere that's going to take care of all the problems. Some of our faculty and I are deluged with children in twos and threes, who as a result of group, class, or school discussions want to follow up with more exploring, more questions. They can't do it in a big group and they're wary of the official tone.

COMMENT: It's hard to keep up on this—not only for me, but for the certain members of my faculty who can establish this person-to-person business. This is *our* particular problem.

COMMENT: I've found that those teachers who are most ready and able to establish rapport with the students on the question of sex are not necessarily the best-qualified people to talk about it at all. On the contrary. And many of those who are best able to speak about it are extremely reticent. If one could bring those people to the point where they would speak about it, they'd have a lot of good things to say. It could easily happen in a faculty that the one least able to speak about sex could be the best able to start the discussion.

COMMENT: Our consulting psychologist comes every other week. Recently he had become aware that more and more youngsters want to talk with him individually about the kinds of problems we have been discussing. He has set up seminars for faculty members, on a voluntary basis. Young faculty members, some of whom might be described as Victorian, come to these sessions in order to find out, first of all, what the biology teacher has been doing, and what the chaplain has been doing in Christian ethics, and also what *they* might be able to do. We think this is going to be of some help.

We also have parents' weekends in the fall and in the spring. This spring we decided to tell the parents in advance that the subject would be "Sex Education: What Do You Parents Want Us to Do About It?" The biology teacher, the chaplain, and I as head will be the panel. We will hopefully get some discussion going among the parents of juniors and seniors. We are not at all sure that they'll be willing to talk, but we hope they will.

COMMENT: There is a good deal of fear within us as we imagine ourselves actually doing what we are talking about, and this probably is getting in the way of our coming to any definite statements as to how to proceed. Then again, we must start somewhere. I wonder how many of us would be willing to face our parents and our students—an artificial situation, obviously, but to dramatize the point let me put it this way—and talk about our honest beliefs, even to talk about our own sexual practices, marital and premarital. If we can acknowledge this fear within us we might be drawn into discussions, into open and frank statements about ourselves. It might clear the air a little.

We are fearful of parental reaction to whatever we might say in the classrooms that might be in defiance of the conventional morality—not the conventional morality that is practiced, because there is little practiced of what is preached—but of conventional preached morality.

We school heads are two persons. We are *the institutional person* and we are *the individual person*. I don't know that I am capable of becoming the individual person in my institutional role, even if I want to be, because as someone pointed out you take on a different image in the students' eyes. To some extent every one of us is forced into playing the role that others cast us in, whether we want to or not.

AFTERWORD

This book ends neither on an inspirational note nor on anybody's testimonial on how to teach sex education. It ends where this conference of educators ended: at the point of a new beginning of individual and group efforts to do something useful in the field of sex education. The book also ends appropriately with the words of an adult, a professional in his field but not an expert in sex education, who is exploring the problem of how to reach young people in some kind of encounter of real persons, rather than simply in a facing of role players.

No one claims to have the last word on sex education or an itemized, packaged program on sex education to offer the world. Surely this is clear from every comment recorded here. 'And eloquently clear is a far wider and deeper range of meanings for the term "sex education" than is usually understood.

The concerns, ideals, bafflements, hopes, dilemmas. and convictions spoken here offer not answers but guides to exploration, not a program but a challenge to create many different programs, suitable to the people and communities making and experiencing them. Surely the voices raised here can join those of concerned adults and young people across the country as we seek ways toward a fuller understanding and expression of our own humanness as men, as women, and as individual persons.

APPENDIX A
SEX EDUCATION PROGRAMS

The following programs represent a variety of approaches. They include some that have been tested over a period of years and others that are new indeed. In every case, those who provided the information did so with hesitation, questioning the value of their contribution to other schools. While it is hoped that the examples of these schools might be helpful to others in designing programs of their own, we caution against selecting any one of the programs described as a model. Each school must develop its own program to meet its particular requirements and expectations. Determination of the latter will necessarily involve careful thought and study.

DESCRIPTION OF A PROGRAM AT A BOYS' SCHOOL IN THE EAST, PREPARED BY THE TEACHER OF THE COURSE

Sex education at our school is presented as an integral part of a year's course in ethics which is given to all eighth graders and all new boys entering Grade 9. Classes meet once a week. Approximately six sessions are devoted to the section on sex. The only text employed is *Life Goes On* by Burnett, Clemenson and Hayman (Harcourt, Brace & Co). This book is used only in the classroom and is not circulated among the student body.

It is important to help a boy learn something about the various emotional adjustments that are required for him to live easily and happily in the inevitable human situations which must be encompassed as he reaches maturity. Once he understands how to begin to manage his ego drive and to adapt it in a reasonable and ethical way to the needs of others, he is at least able to comprehend the meaning of love in its most complete manifestation. A boy cares about being a thoughtful son, a considerate brother, an unselfish friend, or a loyal colleague stands a better chance of being a good husband.

While I can only applaud the gradual lifting of Victorian barriers and an increasing willingness to accept sexual enlightenment as a

127

normal and necessary part of a young man's education, I feel that our enthusiasm to espouse a new concept sometimes obscures our vision. A good deal of the material I have read on sex seems to devote itself to the techniques of achieving coitus perfectus and says little about the sex act as an ultimate expression of love.

Our society is primarily Anglo-Saxon in tradition and essentially monogamous in its concept of marriage. It courts the ideal of fidelity and at least recognizes the virtues of chastity. For the Mediterranean and Oriental, the male attitude toward sex before and after marriage is far more permissive, and until now has been accepted, if not particularly relished, by the female.

Unless we are going to change in a radical manner our prevailing idea of morality and ethical behavior, young men must be given every possible aid in honoring the ideal for which the society in which they will exist is going to hold them responsible. This is why, in the courses I teach, I begin with the study of simple expressions of emotion and with the understanding that the sexual life of a man finds its complete fulfillment in marriage, where it should exist, not as an automatic release of physical desire, but as the climactic expression of the abiding respect, honor, and concern which must be constantly nurtured in any marriage to make it happy and enduring.

In teaching young men, the reward of this ideal must be clearly explained, because in a certain sense the ideal itself is somewhat contrary to nature. The male is easily aroused, quickly satisfied. I should rather talk less about the definite difference of time required to attain a climax, and more about how this most important physical adjustment in marriage can become the prideful responsibility of the male, if he has learned to be sensitive and considerate in the myriad number of other situations which arise when two people live together.

In other words, I am not certain that I should want to teach a course in sex education unless I could spend a considerable amount of time studying the cause and effect of a variety of emotional values which can and should contribute to a complete sexual experience. I have found that from the simple standpoint of achieving the necessary rapport and confidence with my students it is better to begin in this way.

With regard to student reaction, over a ten-year period I have found that an adolescent experiences great relief when he learns that other boys have been living with the same thoughts and feelings which have often troubled him. He is far more willing to talk about this, the most personal part of his life, with a person with whom he has no deep emotional ties, and participation in group discussion gives him confidence. There is the possibility that open and frank discussion may increase a boy's curiosity about his sexual life to the point of defeating the purpose of enlightenment, but there has never been any indication that this is so at our school. Other far more erotic stimuli can easily be found at the local newsstand.

Outline of the Course

ETHICS TERM I

SEPTEMBER
1. An explanation of the ego drive which motivates all aggressiveness and ultimately all creativity and progress.
2. The God idea which controls aggressiveness. The concept of a perfect state of being which acts as a check upon the ego.
3. Frustration—the thwarting of the ego drive—the basis of all difficulties men encounter in living with themselves and others.

OCTOBER
A study of the results of frustration.
1. *Overaggressiveness*—the bully type—manifestations in the home, classroom, and playing field.
2. *Envy and jealousy*—how they relate to overaggressiveness and how they differ. How, because they deflate the ego, they are unnatural.
3. *Untruthfulness*—the product of insecurity, which is a temporary refuge from dissatisfaction.

NOVEMBER
1. *Conceit*—how it differs from self-evaluation and self-respect.
2. *Exhibitionism*—false assurance gained by projection into unreality.
3. *Ridicule*—the easiest and most harmful solution of momentary uncertainty. How it differs from constructive criticism.

TERM II

DECEMBER
Human Relations—The Family
1. Understanding one's parents and achieving happiness with a minimum of the normal friction that is unavoidable in any small, closely knit group. "Generationitis." The responsibilities of a teen-ager to his parents and an appreciation of the benefits derived from a secure family life which is based on mutual trust and respect.
2. The sibling relationship—problems arising among brothers and sisters of various ages. An explanation of the relatitve position in the family of the first child, the middle child, or the only child. How to minimize disagreements and promote better understanding among siblings. Tolerance and loyalty as opposed to petty criticism and envy.

JANUARY

Sex Education

1. *Life Goes On* (Burnett, Clemensen, Hayman. Harcourt, Brace & Co.) The reproductive cycle. Special emphasis is placed on the physical make-up of the young male—the normalcy of increased sexual interest, frequent spontaneous erection, and the function of nocturnal emission. The sublimation of desire by mental control and physical activity. The question of masturbation as a practice which is neither harmful nor sinful, but which is usually unnecessary and, if resorted to frequently, indicative of insecurity, unfulfillment, or unhappiness.

2. The sexual act as an expression of love—its true meaning in the life cycle. A healthy attitude to adopt toward sexual attraction among teen-agers. Dating, and a simple set of rules to follow. Learning to have an emotional control that is reliable. Overseriousness—"puppy" love. Successful social relations with the opposite sex which are based on common interests and participation in group activities.

FEBRUARY

Social Relations

The responsibilities of privilege. Recognition of one's social duties. Learning to understand people who are different from us. The difficult task of "putting oneself in the other person's shoes." The importance of social integrity, and the fact that one's good name is one of his most priceless possessions.

TERM III

MARCH

The Man of Quality—his characteristics and his place in society.

1. *Intelligence*—why the world sets a high price on it and why it must be constantly developed and expanded as the key to all creativity and progress. How education advances civilization.

2. *Honesty*—the difficulties encountered by the idealist in a competitive world. The long-range satisfaction of truthfulness as opposed to the frequent quick rewards of dishonesty.

APRIL

1. *Courage*—the difference between physical and mental courage. Why standing up for what you believe to be right is often a very difficult task. Blind courage as contrasted with intellectual and physical toughness. Why "giving in" is frequently the most demanding kind of courage.

2. *Control*—the goal of maturity. How living in human society from earliest childhood requires the learning of constant physical and mental controls, which add strength and dignity to our lives. Why we basically disrespect the uncontrolled person.

3. *The power of human love*—Family love and physical love having been earlier discussed, the emphasis here is on concern for one's fellow human beings. Why all men and women need love. The necessity of belonging. Loneliness and the need for giving. "Concern" rather than "charity" as an understanding for this kind of love.

MAY

Manners and etiquette—how they are related and how they differ. Manners as a constant revelation of one's character and an instinctive guardian of one's innermost thoughts and feelings.

How good manners function successfully in any social situation and with all types of people. Etiquette as a gracious projection of manners, common only to a given situation.

DESCRIPTION OF 5th-, 10th-, AND 12th-GRADE COURSES TAUGHT AT TWO SCHOOLS IN THE EAST BY DR. ALAN F. GUTTMACHER, PRESIDENT PLANNED PARENTHOOD–WORLD POPULATION

My teaching in sex education below the college level has been confined to five classes per year to fifth graders at one school in Baltimore (1948–52) and five classes per year to high school sophomores and seniors at another school in New York City (1954–   ). Both schools recruit students from sophisticated homes where free discussion and question and answer between household members are the rule. Since I am a physician who through his own research, teaching, and practice has had lifelong contact with the physiology of reproduction, my sex teaching focused on the biological rather than broader sphere of human sexuality. The courses followed quite closely my two books—*Life in the Making*, Viking Press, 1933, and *Into This Universe*, Viking Press, 1937. The former is out of print, but can still be found in many libraries; the latter has passed through many editions and titles. Presently it is extensively revised under the title *Pregnancy and Birth*, a paperback of the New American Library.

My general purpose is to detoxify the topic of sex, to remove creation from the realm of pornography. I try to accomplish it by treating the topic scientifically, factually, not brazenly but without any vestige of embarrassment. I encourage all and any questions at any time and field each question with enthusiasm, sometimes turning the question to suit the purpose of the group, rather than the individual. I always use the scientific name for organs, often at the same time giving the lay equivalent.

Fifth Grade (five class sessions)

1. Importance of reproduction for perpetuation of species.
2. Advantages of sexual over asexual reproduction—former bestows variation on progeny. Even some asexual organisms have occasional cycles of sexual reproduction.
3. Evolution of the process of mating with examples: (a) starfish—no propinquity or physical awareness between male and female; (b) king salmon—the dramatic sojourn to headwaters, awareness but no physical contact, cooperation in scooping out nest and covering eggs; (c) frog—not only awareness between sexes but physical contact, male clasp organ, external fertilization; (d) mammalian pattern and pattern of many sub-mammalian species—internal fertilization, least wasteful of germ cells.
4. The male and female reproductive organs, anatomy and physiology, role of hormones in sexual behavior.
5. Demonstrate the internal reproductive organs of pregnant dead lab rat, showing fetuses, placenta, ovaries, etc. Incise scrotum of recently killed male rat, removing testicles, demonstrating motile spermatozoa under the microscope.
6. Discuss differences in reproduction between humans and animals.
   (a) Litter size, general biological factors influencing it, human twins.
   (b) Helpless state of human young compared to sheep, horse, etc.
   (c) Advantages of perpetual union of male and female in protection and training of young.
   (d) Differences between human male and female.
       (1) Puberty.
       (2) Menstruation—normal, range of variations, hygiene of dysmenorrhoea.
       (3) Masturbation.
       (4) Seminal emissions.
7. Pregnancy and birth.
   (a) Fertilization.
   (b) Duration of pregnancy, span of difference between 11 day duration of opossum and 24 month of whale yet eggs same size. In humans—all ethnic groups have the same duration of pregnancy. Birth weight of newborn differ—white, black, yellow. One species —therefore all mankind fertile with each other.
   (c) Growth of fetus.
   (d) Birth process.
Show preserved human fetuses of eight weeks, three and six months. For pregnancy and labor—illustrations in *Dickinson Birth Atlas*.

Typical questions of 11-year-olds

1. Do people have coitus only to make babies?
2. Can one swim or do athletics during menstruation?
3. Why does pregnancy last a certain number of days or months?
4. Can you tell when you are going to start menstruating?
5. Does menstruation weaken one? How much blood is lost?
6. Is there a way of making a boy baby or a girl baby?
7. Are wet dreams harmful? How do you stop them?
8. Can one tell whether a boy or girl is going to be fertile when they grow up?
9. How young can a girl or boy be to become a parent?
10. Tell me about undescended testicles.
11. Are menstruation in the human and a heat period in a dog or cat the same?
12. Why does a man have so many sperm cells and a woman just one egg?
13. Do you approve of young marriages?
14. What is contraception?

Sophomore and Senior Classes (five 40-minute periods)

1. Maleness and femaleness, chromosomal differences cause hormonal differences, eunuchoid state, animal experimentation, behavioral pattern altered by castration, effects eliminated by gonad transplants or replacement injections.
2. Differences between species in mating patterns.
   (a) Monestrous, e.g. seal, bear.
   (b) Polyestrous—sheep, rats, cats and dogs. Effects of domestication.
   (c) Constant willingness to mate with fluctuations of interest, particularly in female, all primates. Origin, advantages.
3. Reproductive anatomy of human male and female, menstrual cycle, ovulation, menopause. Is there a male climacteric?
4. Process of copulation
   (a) Mechanics of erection, ejaculation, detumescence.
   (b) Hymen, distensibility of vagina.
   (c) Emotional reaction, erogenous zones, intimacy of lovemaking, civilized pattern.
5. Sex mores in modern world, continence, fidelity, etc.
6. Abnormal sexual behavior—homosexuality, fetishes.
7. Fertilization.
   (a) Process, site, the ovum, spermatozoa.

(b) How chances can be enhanced, fertile cycle days.

(c) How chances can be diminished. Contraception, detailed discussion of methods; sterilization.

8. Infertility—frequency, causes, therapy.

9. Pregnancy, litter size, human multiple births, pregnancy duration, development of fetus, physiology of intrauterine life, fetal activities —movements, respiration, voiding, etc. Prenatal care.

10. Abortion—spontaneous, induced; therapeutic and illegal. Need to revise laws. Illegitimacy.

11. Labor—caesarean section, "natural" childbirth versus medicated.

12. Newborn—weight, length, racial variations, mortality, malformations—genetic causes; postconceptional causes—German measles, etc. Prematurity. Birth injury—central nervous system damage.

13. Lactation—hormonal basis, breast versus bottle.

14. Factors affecting: spacing of children and family size. Ideal—babies by choice rather than chance.

15. Age of marriage. Advantages and disadvantages of youthful marriage. Teen-age divorce rates. Value of postponing children until education of parents completed. Chief ally of successful pregnancy —youth.

16. Population dynamics. Birth rate minus death rate yields rate of natural increase (B.R. − D.R. = N.I.R.) Growth of world population from Ptolemies to A.D. 2000. Population growth in various countries, industrialized versus developing. Current U.S. picture. Problems associated with rapid growth—distortion of age pyramid, educational and health demands, food production, depletion of natural resources, G.N.P. (gross national product), and per capita income. Malthus—impractical solution, moral restraint. Practical solutions—contraception, sterilization, and abortion.

Typical questions of high school sophomores and seniors.

1. Is it harmful to remain chaste indefinitely?
2. Does masturbation cause physical or mental illness?
3. Is the birth control pill harmless?
4. Do you approve of Tampax for young girls?
5. Is there a true difference in heavy petting and going the limit?
6. Are all the eggs in an ovary present at birth?
7. Do the two ovaries alternate each month in discharging an egg?
8. Does continence improve athletic ability, for example, during training?
9. What is artificial insemination?
10. Is abortion always dangerous?

11. Must there always be true intercourse to cause a pregnancy?
12. Is sterilization a permanent procedure?
13. Do you favor premarital intercourse?
14. Is masturbation harmful? How do you stop it?
15. Can a woman tell when she ovulates and which ovary was involved?
16. Is there any way to tell right away whether an intercourse caused pregnancy?
17. Have pimples anything to do with sex?

FROM A HEADMASTER OF A BOYS' SCHOOL IN THE EAST

We establish initially and clearly that when we are talking about sex we are talking about manhood and womanhood. The basic questions have little to do with the facts of reproduction. They have to do with what it means to be a man, and with what it means to be a woman.

Whoever is programming sex education for a school is going to miss the boat unless he defines this ground at the outset. Unquestionably the anxieties about sex activity which strain adolescents are relevant. They can be explored in the context of sexuality, and children should not feel cheated. But any program ought to begin on ground that is higher than they are accustomed in their thought and general discussion of the subject of sex.

In our program sex and sexuality are considered in the context of our chaplain's senior religion course. One year he and his counterpart at a nearby seminary for girls had some informal evening discussions in which boys and girls participated with adults.

These are the basic ingredients of our program: (1) discussion in the context of the classroom (presumably a class which concerns itself chiefly with values); (2) full-dress confrontation of the entire group by someone who can speak with authority, breadth of background, and moral conviction; and (3) informal conversation by boys and girls together, in small groups, with adult participation. Obviously the adult must be intellectually and temperamentally capable of making constructive conversation with children on the subject of sex.

REVIEW OF A PROGRAM OF SEX EDUCATION IN A BOYS' SCHOOL IN CANADA

For eight years I have given a course in sex education to boys in grade seven at an independent school in a large city. There are three grades seven, with approximately twenty-five boys in each class.

Each of the three classes receives one period of forty minutes per week. The ordinary pressures of school life are deliberately removed. There is no homework, no written tasks, no tests. Conscious effort is made to permit a relaxed and informal atmosphere, free from any form of anxiety.

Attendance is voluntary. In eight years, however, only one boy has not taken part, the result of his father's request for exemption. In no other instance has a boy willingly absented himself from the class.

At this level, the course is simple and straightforward. The boys are given a candid explanation of the reproductive systems, both male and female. Clear, uncomplicated visual aids are used. Detailed minutiae are given later in their high school studies in biology.

The course stresses a relaxed, sensible, and unself-conscious approach to the study of sex. Generous time is devoted to answering questions of the boys. There is no specific text; the teacher follows a list of topics and offers verbal and visual explanations.

Emphasis upon group participation, straightforward approach, and teacher attitude helps to lessen self-consciousness. Any sign of uncertainty on the part of the teacher would be catastrophic. Either the teacher is prepared or is not prepared to deal with sex education. There can be no place for reservation, self-doubt, or compromise.

A question box is available in each class, for unsigned questions. At the beginning of each period, the box is opened and questions within are answered.

At this level of pre-adolescence, the main objectives of the program are to prepare the boy for future physical changes and to stress positive values related to personal conduct. The course is deliberately not too closely constructed, so that a wide range of questions can be answered. There are no set limits or boundaries. Any question asked is answered. Questions posed most frequently deal with sexual intercourse, masturbation, seminal emission, prostitution, venereal disease, and physical freaks. The course approach is both technical and cultural. Religious belief is not discussed, and the boys, when necessary, are instructed to seek advice from their parents or church on this subject.

Sequence of Topics

1. General introduction to course.
   Review of attitudes toward sex over the years.
   Stress on normal relaxed atmosphere.
   Questionnaire to determine who have had sex instruction.
2. Discussion of growing up to be a "gentleman." Discussion of such virtues as honesty, courtesy, loyalty, etc.

3. Discussion of three basic drives, i.e., thirst, hunger, and sex.
4. Puberty and adolescence.
   Characteristics of boys.
   Characteristics of girls.
5. Female sex organs.
6. Male sex organs.
7. Female reproductive system.
   Outline of menstruation.
   Outline of pregnancy.
8. Male reproductive system.
   Outline of seminal emissions.
9. Sexual intercourse.
10. Masturbation.
11. Homosexuality and lesbianism.
12. Menopause, sterility, impotence.
13. Circumcision.
14. Venereal disease.
15. Birth cycle, caesarean section, abortion.
16. Twins.
    Identical.
    Non-identical.
17. Review of terms.
18. Final questionnaire.

THE HOME, THE SCHOOL, AND SEX EDUCATION
BY ERIC W. JOHNSON, VICE PRINCIPAL
GERMANTOWN FRIENDS SCHOOL, PHILADELPHIA

Before I specify the program at our school, I want to set forth nine basic propositions which I think we must all keep in mind as we think about sex education and which we should teach at some time during the program:
1. Sexuality is not the same thing as genitality, but many people confuse the two. The differences between male and female are much greater than the differences between their bodies. Many of the differences are culturally derived.
2. Sex is not a disease; it is a good and powerful part of humanity. Sex need not be discussed only by doctors and psychiatrists.
3. Sex does not have to be, as Dr. Mary Steichen Calderone, executive director of the Sex Information and Education Council of the U.S. (SIECUS) says, "either an orgy or a sacrament." It is a part of the

fantasy of our society to present it as one or the other. Sex is a complex, subtle, and often difficult set of relationships.

4. Coitus is only one of the many ways a person may express his sexuality. Many expressions of sex include both the mind and the spirit; sometimes the body is hardly involved at all.

5. It is not physically harmful to refrain from physical sexual activity, or to postpone it until one is mature enough for it and all of its consequences. The need for sexual outlet is not like the needs for food, air, water, or elimination of body waste; none of these latter needs can be denied very long without causing death.

6. Animal sex and human sex are very different. Most animals copulate only when they are ready to procreate, and their behavior is controlled by instinct. The human sexual desire has little relationship to readiness for procreation, and human sexual behavior differs vastly among different individuals and different societies. Most animal sex is only a matter of body; human sex involves the whole being and is, to a great extent, determined by upbringing and culture.

7. Sex education is thus not just education about human reproduction. It is not mere biology. It is, rather, sociology and human relations.

8. Individuals mature at different rates; some have much stronger sex drives than others; some are more interested in sex than in almost anything else, while others are, at the same period of their lives, quite uninterested.

9. People have strong feelings about sexual behavior, both their own and that of others. This is especially true of adults observing teen-agers. Adults can easily be offended, outraged, shocked, or frightened. (So can teen-agers.) There are questions of good taste involved, of manners, of consideration for the convictions of others. There is a distinction to be learned between the sort of behavior appropriate in a public place and that appropriate in private.

As we plan our sex education program, we should keep in mind that a single exposure to sex education is not enough. Different individuals will absorb and benefit from different aspects of sex education at different ages. Thus, a sex education program must be flexible and must extend over a span of years.

We must remember also that teen-agers will rarely admit to adults whom they know well, and often not to each other, their ignorance about sexual matters. Often they do not know they are ignorant, believing that as soon as they have been informed about what sexual intercourse is they know it all. (Many adults, even married ones, are ignorant, too). Most teen-agers, somehow, find it self-demeaning to admit they have a lot of questions and are worried and puzzled about a lot of things concerning sex.

If sex education is to be effective, we must level with our teen-agers about sex. They want all the information, plainly and realistically presented. Full information is the first prerequisite of responsible behavior. Preaching and exhortation will not work today, although adolescents want to know where respected adults stand. They want this as a part of their information and as a guide, not as a prescription. They are, however, very much interested in discussing the moral questions connected with sex, and they are anxious to develop a moral code of their own.

The sex education program at Germantown Friends School takes into account fairly well, I think, the considerations I have suggested above. Specifically, here is what we do:

Grade 6: The lower school science teacher shows the film *Human Growth* to boys and girls together, after parents have had a chance to view it previously. The film deals with the facts of human reproduction, although it is not explicit about coitus. It does not deal with the social problems of sex. Immediately after the film, in an informal session, the teacher answers questions the children have. Usually there is not more than one session.

Grade 8: The head of the junior high school, a teacher of social studies, includes a discussion of sex as an outgrowth of an over-all study of Asia. Consideration of the population explosion leads to a discussion of birth control which, in turn, leads to reading and discussion of sex and sexuality. Each section is divided into boys and girls so that discussions may be frank. My book, *Love and Sex in Plain Language,* is required reading. Sometimes a film is shown (either *Human Growth* or *Human Reproduction*); the basic physical facts are reviewed, and then the group gets into the moral and cultural aspects of sex. This discussion is based on questions raised by the students. There are about four sessions for each group.

Grade 10: Near the beginning of the school year, the boys and girls meet separately for four sessions, the boys with a professor of psychiatry at the University of Pennsylvania and psychiatric consultant to a number of schools and to the Marriage Council of Philadelphia; the girls with a former assistant dean at Penn, now Director of Continuing Education for Women, who worked for a number of years with the Philadelphia Marriage Council. Usually the first session is devoted to finding out how much the students know and to answering factual questions. Students then write down any questions they may have, and the succeeding sessions are based on these and whatever questions come up in discussion. The hope is that the students will discuss fully what is most on their minds.

Grade 12: The procedure is exactly the same as with the tenth grade. However, the students are two years older, and within a year almost all will be in college.

In some years, after the sessions in grades 10 and 12, each student completes anonymously a brief questionnaire evaluating the sessions. Almost all advocate they be continued for future classes. A few pooh-pooh the sessions as old hat and useless, stating that they learned little. Many more say that they find them of some value.

Other aspects of our program: Throughout the lower school, the children observe various animals in various stages of reproduction. This gives a valuable perspective, but it is not the same thing as educating about human sex. Whenever children in our rather informal elementary school science classes ask questions about human sex, the teacher answers factually and plainly. Usually the questions concern the physical aspects of sex. In grades 10 and 12, the biology courses teach about reproduction, both animal and human.

Further, throughout the school, the English, anthropology, and history courses deal with problems of human existence and human relationships, and often with the relationships between men and women. In the broadest sense, such studies of the nature and experiences of human beings are a part of sex education and help create a healthy, understanding sexual orientation.

Thus, at several levels and from several points of view, the school teaches boys and girls about human sexuality and its responsible use. The subject matter is basically the same, but the approach and interest are different in different grades. In each of the four grades, 6, 8, 10, and 12, there is an opportunity for free and full discussion, which no book or lecture can provide.

At different levels and in different ways, a variety of related topics are treated: sexual intercourse, conception and contraception, pregnancy and birth, necking and petting, menstruation, masturbation, venereal disease, sexual deviations. Basic questions are raised: What are the purposes of sex? When are people ready for it? Should there be rules about sexual conduct? If so, who should make them and how should they be enforced? What are the results of sexual activity, good and bad?

Students have a chance to express their personal worries, either directly or indirectly through questions: Am I normal? Am I adequate? Am I oversexed? Am I undersexed? Are my thoughts evil? Am I desirable?

How should I behave at parties and on dates? What will I face in college?

It is rarely possible for parents and their children to have free, full, open discussions about sex and sexual behavior. They know each other too well. I am sure that parents ought to make themselves available for discussion. They should, if they can, find opportunities to give information and to answer questions, if any come or can be invited. Perhaps they can offer a book to read and then discuss the book. But parents should not be worried if their efforts are rebuffed. They should remain open and not feel resentful. The most important things parents can provide are: an example of married satisfaction, with physical, intellectual, and spiritual sharing and warmth; an unreserved amount of love and support for their children; plenty of time, care, and attention for each child; and discipline, lovingly and consistently applied. From such homes, even if there is no specific sex education, are likely to come secure, warm children, prepared to participate maturely in the world of sex.

In school, there is a great advantage, especially in the upper grades, in having an outsider teach sex education. Teen-agers are usually better able to discuss sex freely with a warm, understanding, well-informed person who has no connection with the discipline and structure of the school or the home. They reveal their deepest thoughts and most burning questions about sex to the nonjudging adult whom they are not likely ever to see again, and who cannot possibly be shocked or use against them anything they may say. That is why we use outside consultants, and why no one from the school is ever present at the sessions.

A sex education program, no matter how thorough and enlightened, is not a panacea. It will never, by itself, solve all the problems of human behavior, although it will help. A greedy, ruthless, exploitative, hate-filled, or insecure person may continue to be just such a person after his sex education, and his sexual behavior may continue to exhibit these characteristics. But even such a person, through sex education, will gain insight into himself and into the consequences, both good and bad, of different sorts of sexual behavior.

Perhaps the most important aspect of sex education, as of all education which attempts to affect behavior, is that the individual is helped to create for himself an ideal and a set of values. We hope that these will include respect for self and one's powers; equal respect for others and consideration of their welfare; an understanding of the need to postpone immediate gratification for ultimate greater reward; social usefulness; and marriage and a family, within which human sexual experiences, I believe, are most fruitfully developed.

FOR: THE HEAD OF THE SCHOOL
BY JOHN CHANDLER, JR., CONSULTANT
NATIONAL ASSOCIATION OF INDEPENDENT SCHOOLS

How should a school go about planning a program of sex education? What constitutes a sound program? These questions have been directed to me by a good number of school heads. Until now I have parried them because I was not at all sure of the validity of my tentative answers and did not wish to risk starting schools off on a doubtful course. The truth of the matter is that few schools, public or independent, have had sufficient experience with sex education to feel sure of their ground, and those that have been at it the longest are the first to caution that what works for them might be completely unworkable in another situation. The variety of practice noted among the schools with programs confirms this and suggests that it will be a long time before anyone will be in a position to offer answers to these questions with any degree of confidence.

There is now no one right way to proceed with the planning of a program. Nor is there any one program that can be cited as sound in all respects. Each school must tackle the questions on its own, searching for answers most appropriate for its particular circumstances.

Having said this, let me proceed to set down here the tentative answers that I have given to those who have backed me into a corner and said, "That's all very well, but what would you do if you were us?"

Having first convinced myself that the school had a responsibility for sex education, I would:

1. Initiate a program of reading and general discussion within the faculty, encouraging the participation of faculty wives and husbands.

2. Appoint a special committee of those faculty members most interested and likely to be involved in the program, including representation from the school's medical staff and, if a day school, from the Board of Trustees and the parent body. The committee's charge would be to define the particular needs of the school and its students and to design a program to meet these needs. In the course of its deliberations the committee should:

a. Examine the programs of other schools, and if possible arrange discussion with those who have had firsthand experience with sex education.

b. Bring students from the highest grade in the school into the discussion. Let them help decide what should be done, what they would have liked to have had; what specific knowledge they have missed; what their concerns and questions are about values and relationships.

c. Examine available teaching materials—texts, films, discussion guides.

3. When the program is set and before it is initiated, I would take special care to be sure:

a. That the entire faculty and all parents understand its purpose and aim.

b. That parents are given specific information on what is to be taught.

c. That parents have an opportunity to see the films and examine whatever books or other materials will be used.

Note: A number of schools have successfully begun a program *before* informing parents, presenting them in due course with a *fait accompli*. They chose this approach to avoid what they feared might be an endless debate if the parent body was given an opportunity to express its opinion before the program was under way. As no school has yet reported anything but strong support from parents regardless of when they were informed, it may well be that one approach is as good as another, but my choice would be to inform—not to ask for approval, but to explain what was to be done and why—parents in advance.

As to the program itself, I shall limit myself to a discussion of basic principles on which there appears to be general agreement and add one or two personal observations.

A carefully planned program of sex education will have two essential elements:

1. The provision of knowledge—the facts of human physiology and reproduction to be transmitted systematically as children progress through school, different aspects at different ages in keeping with their capacity to understand.

2. Opening the door to honest and free discussion between adults and children of the latter's concerns and questions about sex and sexual behavior. The first step to this end is removal of the long-standing taboo that has made discussion of sex all but impossible. As adults have lived with this taboo longer than children, it will be more difficult for them to make the adjustment in their attitudes towards the subject which will permit them to initiate discussion of it. Responsibility for opening the door rests with the older generation, and the young can be counted on to respond promptly and eagerly when the opportunity is provided.

Presumably, in the long run, both 1 and 2 will be accomplished through a natural progression of teaching and discussion from kindergarten through the twelfth grade. The immediate problem, however, is to decide what should and can be done right away for the children at various age levels who for the most part have had little of either. The greatest concern is clearly for those in the higher grades. What is done for them will necessarily be less than ideal. Perhaps the most we can expect to do for seniors and juniors is give them a quick refresher course on the "facts," provide answers to their specific questions about sex, and let them know that we are aware of their concerns about sexual behavior and would like to offer whatever help and advice we can, should they wish to discuss them with us.

At whatever age, the provision of knowledge is a relatively simple and straightforward matter. But to guide children to a full understanding of themselves as sexual beings and to prepare them to deal with sex responsibly and intelligently is a far more complex and sensitive undertaking and involves a great deal more than is implied by the term "sex education." A partial listing of topics included in one school's program for grades seven through nine will indicate the dimensions of the task.

Physical growth—patterns and individual differences.

The sex drive—differences between male and female.

Relationships with the opposite sex—responsibilities of each toward the other.

Charting one's course in life—establishing one's own value system and moral code.

Understanding peer group pressures and their influence, good and bad.

Understanding the expectations of parents.

What a particular school will include in its program and how it will go about both giving instruction and opening the door to discussion can only be determined, it seems to me, after the school has defined the nature and extent of its responsibility for sex education. Obviously, this definition will vary according to whether the school is day or boarding, one sex or coeducational, secondary or elementary, and will be influenced by such considerations as the degree of sophistication of the student body, the standards of social conduct in the community from which they come, the expectations of parents, and many others.

Who is qualified to teach and/or lead discussion? Here again, I offer what I believe to be the consensus of those who have had experience, namely, that any person whom youngsters respect and in whom they have confidence and trust, and who can meet them where they are with frankness and honesty, and can discuss their concerns objectively and nonjudgmentally with them, is eligible. Obviously, no one should attempt it who does not feel entirely comfortable with the subject or has any doubts about his capacity to handle forthrightly and without prejudice any and all questions that may come up. Criteria such as age, sex, or marital status are relatively unimportant.

Every school has on its faculty people who answer to this description and who could be prepared, or prepare themselves, to give instruction and guide discussion. Becoming "comfortable" is largely a matter of getting used to the vocabulary and shedding the restraints which have hampered adults for several generations and this should happen in the normal course of the discussion that leads to the planning of a program. The basic knowledge required is not so complex that it cannot be acquired through reading, supplemented by a session or two with the school doctor to clarify any points in doubt.

Most schools will undoubtedly rely on a doctor or another qualified professional to provide instruction for older students in the specifics of reproduction, contraception, and so forth and to answer their technical questions, which are almost sure to range beyond the capacity of the best-prepared teacher. The faculty may or may not be able, in time, to take over this particular responsibility, but it seems clear that they can, and highly desirable that they should, be prepared to guide discussion of values and behavior with both older and younger students, and also to undertake the instruction of the younger in the rudiments of sex. The professional, while obviously the best-qualified to discuss the specifics, may not be the best person to lead a group discussion of values and behavior. And even if he has the interest in and understanding of young people that would so qualify him, it is unlikely that he could give the time necessary. Whatever the extent of the professional's involvement, the important thing is that the faculty know precisely what he has covered so that they may be prepared to deal with the students demand for further discussion which is sure to follow his departure.

For those who may be tempted to put sex entirely in the hands of the professional, an additional point: If his contact with the school is only occasional, his visits to deal with sex will keep the subject in a special category and maintain its status as a topic that cannot be discussed except with him and by him, with the obvious result that the taboo on sex will remain firmly fixed and the door to communication between students and faculty as tightly shut as it has always been.

The consensus is, I believe, that in the long run a program in sex education can best be conducted by and within the school itself as a natural and integral part of its total program of instruction and guidance. The professional may be relied upon until the faculty are prepared to step in, and he will obviously continue to serve an important function even after the program is established as an adviser to the faculty and as the person to whom students may go, or be referred, for private discussion of their intimate personal concerns. But if we can eventually reach the point where sex is regarded not as a "problem," but as a normal, natural, and vital part of everyone's life, does it not seem logical that youngsters should turn for advice and counsel to normal, natural, and stable adults whom they know well and who know them equally well and are readily available to them? However concerned the professional may be, he cannot possibly know the students as well as the faculty does, nor is he likely to be around when questions or concerns arise.

It is vitally important that we approach sex and any program of sex education from a positive rather than a negative point of view. Following this line of thought, I would suggest that we avoid putting sex education in the same category with education about drugs, alcohol, and tobacco, which are specific threats to health, and, unlike sex, have no positive side, have nothing good to contribute to life.

Sex is essentially a positive force in life. Youngsters should be led to appreciate what is good, fine, and healthy about it and to understand how their sexual powers can be directed to bring them fulfillment and satisfaction. The older generation, I am afraid, tends to lose sight of the bright side in its preoccupation with and emphasis upon the consequences of irresponsible sexual behavior. Surely children should understand that sex is subject to misuse and exploitation and that its power may have negative as well as positive results, but it would be most unfortunate if the negative aspects were to dominate our thinking. It seems far wiser to proceed on the assumption that it is the natural instinct of the young to seek out the good in life and thus that we should help them in every way we can to define and then to realize that which is truly good—in all aspects of living, including sex.

APPENDIX B
RESOURCE AGENCIES IN
THE UNITED STATES

American Home Economics Association
1600 Twentieth Street, N.W.
Washington, D.C.

American Institute of Family Relations
Dr. Paul Popenoe, Director
5287 Sunset Boulevard
Los Angeles, California

American Medical Association
535 North Dearborn Street
Chicago, Illinois

American Social Health Association
Mrs. Elizabeth S. Force, Director of Family Life Education
1790 Broadway
New York 19, New York

Children's Bureau
U.S. Department of Health, Education and Welfare
300 Independence Avenue, S.W.
Washington, D.C.

Child Study Association of America
9 East Eighty-ninth Street
New York 28, New York

Family Life Publications, Inc.
Box 6725
Durham, North Carolina

Maternity Center Association
48 East Ninety-second Street
New York 28, New York

National Council on Family Relations
1219 University Avenue, S.E.
Minneapolis, Minnesota

Sex Information and Education Council of the U.S. (SIECUS)
Mary S. Calderone, M.D., Executive Director
1855 Broadway
New York, New York 10023

E. C. Brown Trust
200 S.W. Alder Street
Portland, Oregon

BIBLIOGRAPHY

BOOKS FOR ADULTS

BARUCH, DOROTHY, *New Ways in Sex Education*, Bantam, 1959.

CALDERONE, M.S., *Adolescent Sexual Behavior*, reprinted from the *National PTA Magazine*. (PP–WP #768).

———, *Health Education for Responsible Parenthood: Preliminary Considerations*, reprinted from *American Journal of Public Health*, Vol. 54, No. 10, October, 1964, pp. 1735–1740. (PP–WP #775).

———, *Married Teen-ager*, reprinted from the *Journal of the International College of Surgeons*, Vol. 43, No. 4, April, 1965.

———, "Sexual Energy—Constructive or Destructive," *Western Journal of Surgery, Obstetrics and Gynecology*, 71:272–277, Nov.–Dec., 1963. (PP–WP #736).

Child Study Association of America. *Facts of Life for Children*, Bobbs-Merrill, 1954.

———, *What to Tell Your Children about Sex*, Duell, 1958.

DAVIS, MAXINE, *Sex and the Adolescent*, Permabooks, 1960.

DESCHIN, CLIA, *Teenagers and Venereal Disease*, U.S. Department of Health, Education and Welfare, 1961.

DUVALL, SYLVANUS and EVELYN, *Sex Ways in Fact and Faith*, Association Press, 1961.

DUVALL, EVELYN, *Love and the Facts of Life*, Association Press, 1961.

ECKERT, RALPH G., *Sex Attitudes in the Home*, Popular Library, 1963.

FLANAGAN, GERALDINE, *The First Nine Months of Life*, Simon & Schuster, 1962.

FRAIBERG, SELMA, *The Magic Years*, Scribner, 1959.

FRANK, MARY and LAWRENCE K., *Your Adolescent at Home and in School,* Viking, 1956. New American Library.

GITTELSOHN, RABBI ROLAND, *Consecrated Unto Me,* Union of American Hebrew Congregations, 1965.

GOTTLIEB, BERNHART, *What a Boy Should Know About Sex,* Bobbs-Merrill, 1961.

———, *What a Girl Should Know About Sex,* Bobbs-Merrill, 1961.

Group for the Advancement of Psychiatry, *Sex and the College Student,* Mental Health Materials Center, 1965.

GREELEY, ANDREW M., *Strangers in the House,* Sheed and Ward, 1961.

GRUNWALD, HENRY ANATOLE, Editor, *Sex in America,* Bantam, 1964.

GUTTMACHER, ALAN, *Pregnancy and Birth,* Signet Key, 1964.

GUTTMACHER, ALAN, and others, *Planning Your Family,* Macmillan, 1963.

Health Education Services, *The Gift of Life,* Mental Health Materials Center, 1951.

HERON, A., Editor, *Toward a Quaker View of Sex,* Friends Bookstore, Revised edition, 1964.

JOHNSON, ERIC W., *How to Live Through Junior High School,* Lippincott, 1959.

JOHNSON, WARREN, *Human Sex and Sex Education,* Macmillan, 1963.

KIRKENDALL, LESTER A., *Sex and Our Society,* Public Affairs Committee, 1964.

———, *Pre-Marital Intercourse and Interpersonal Relations,* Julian Press, 1961.

LERRIGO, MARION O., and SOUTHARD, HELEN, *Facts Aren't Enough,* National Education Association, 1955.

———, *How, When and What to Tell Your Child about Sex,* Dutton, 1956.

LEVINE, MILTON I., and SELIGMANN, JEAN H., *Helping Boys and Girls Understand Their Sex Roles,* Science Research Associates, 1953.

Maternity Center Association, *A Baby Is Born,* Grosset and Dunlap, 1964.

PIKE, JAMES A., *Teen-agers and Sex,* Prentice-Hall, 1965.

REISS, IRA, *Pre-Marital Sexual Standards in America,* Free Press, 1960.

RICHMAN, T. LEFOY, *Venereal Disease,* Public Affairs Committee, 1959.

RIDENOUR, NINA E., and JOHNSON, ISABEL, *Some Special Problems of Children Aged Two to Five,* Child Study Association, 1966.

SATTLER, HENRY, *Parents, Children and the Facts of Life,* Doubleday Image Book, 1956.

SCHEINFELD, AMRAM, *The Human Heredity Book,* Lippincott, 1956.

SCHWARTZ, WILLIAM, *Teacher's Handbook on Venereal Disease,* Education, NEA Publications, 1965.

SPOCK, BENJAMIN, and LERRIGO, MARION O., *Caring for Your Disabled Child,* Macmillan, 1965.

BOOKS FOR CHILDREN AND YOUNG PEOPLE
Ages five to nine

GRUENBERG, SIDONIE M., *The Wonderful Story of How You Were Born,* Doubleday, revised edition, 1959.

LEVINE, MILTON J., and SELIGMANN, *A Baby Is Born,* Golden Press, revised edition, 1962.

Ages nine to twelve

GRUENBERG, BENJAMIN C., and SIDONIE M., *The Wonderful Story of You,* Garden City Books, 1960.

JOHNSON, ERIC W., *Love and Sex in Plain Language,* Lippincott, 1965.

LERRIGO, MARION O., and SOUTHARD, HELEN, in consultation with Milton J. E. Senn, M.D., *A Story About You: The Facts You Want to Know About Sex,* Dutton, 1956.

LERRIGO, MARION O., and CASSIDY, DR. M. A., *A Doctor Talks to 9- to 12-Year-Olds,* Budlong Press, 1964.

LEVINE, MILTON I., M.D., and SELIGMANN, JEAN H., *The Wonder of Life,* Simon & Schuster, 1952.

POWER, JULES, *How Life Begins,* Simon and Schuster, 1965.

Ages thirteen to fifteen

Growing Up and Liking It, Personal Products Company, 1964.

In cooperation with the Chicago Museum of Science and Industry, and the University of Illinois Professional Colleges, *The Miracle of Growth,* Pyramid Books, 1959.

KELIHER, ALICE V., *Life and Growth,* Appleton-Century-Crofts, 1941.

LERRIGO, MARION O., and SOUTHARD, HELEN, *What's Happening to Me?* Dutton, 1956.

WILLIAMS, MARY MCGEE, and KANE, IRENE, *On Becoming a Woman,* Dell, 1959.

World of a Girl, Scott Paper Company, 1965.

Older adolescent and young adult

BOLL, ELEANOR S., *The Man That You Marry,* Macrae Smith, 1963.

BOLL, ELEANOR S., and BOSSARD, JAMES H. S. *The Girl That You Marry,* Macrae Smith, 1960.

DUVALL, EVELYN MILLIS, and HILL, REUBEN, *When You Marry*, Association Press, 1962.

KRICH, ARON, *Facts of Love and Marriage for Young People*, Dell, 1960.

LERRIGO, MARION O., and SOUTHARD, HELEN, in consultation with Milton J. E. Senn, M.D., *Learning About Love: Sound Facts and Healthy Attitudes Toward Sex and Marriage*, Dutton, 1956.

————, *Finding Yourself*, National Education Association, 1955.

LEVINSOHN, FLORENCE, and KELLY, DR. G. LOMBARD, *What Teenagers Want to Know*, Budlong Press, 1962.

SAKOL, JEANNE, *What About Teen-Age Marriage?* Messner, 1961.

RESEARCH

HARTMAN, CARL G., *100 Unanswered Questions*, reprinted from *McCall's*, September, 1964. (PP–WP #763).

NELSON, W. O., M.D., *Physiology of Reproduction and Its Relation to the Regulation of Fertility, Marriage and Family Living*, Vol. XXV, No. 1, February, 1963. (PP–WP #733).

PAMPHLETS

American Medical Association
535 North Dearborn Street
Chicago, Illinois *(Inquire about Sex Education Series)*

Public Affairs Pamphlets
22 East Thirty-eighth Street
New York 16, New York

Science Research Associates
57 West Grand Avenue
Chicago 10, Illinois

The Child Study Association of America
132 East Seventy-fourth Street
New York 21, New York

American Social Health Association
1855 Broadway
New York, New York 10023

SIECUS
1855 Broadway
New York, New York 10023

FILMS

"A Quarter Million Teenagers" (Venereal disease), 16 minutes
Churchill Films
662 North Robinson Boulevard
Los Angeles, California 90069

"Boy to Man" (Physical changes), 16 minutes
Churchill Films
662 North Robinson Boulevard
Los Angeles, California

"From Generation to Generation" (Reproductive process), 30 minutes
McGraw-Hill
330 West Forty-second Street
New York 32, New York

"Girl to Woman" (Physical changes)
Churchill Films
6671 Sunset Boulevard
Los Angeles, California

"How Do I Love Thee" (Premarital sex), 20 minutes
Brigham Young University
Provo, Utah

"Human Beginnings" (Reproduction education), 20 minutes
E. C. Brown Trust
220 S.W. Alder
Portland, Oregon

"Human Growth" (Reproduction education), 20 minutes
E. C. Brown Trust
220 S.W. Alder
Portland, Oregon

"Human Reproduction" (Reproduction education)
McGraw-Hill
330 West Forty-second Street
New York 32, New York

"Phoebe" (Premarital pregnancy), 29 minutes
National Film Board of Canada
620 Fifth Avenue
New York 20, New York

Sale through:
McGraw-Hill Text Film Division
330 West Forty-second Street
New York 32, New York
Rented from:
Contemporary Films
614 Davis Street
Evanston, Illinois

"The Innocent Party" (Syphilis), 18 minutes
Calvin Company
1105 Truman Road
Kansas City 6, Missouri

"Worth Waiting For" (Early marriage), 20 minutes
Brigham Young University
Provo, Utah

"It's Wonderful Being a Girl" (Menstruation for 5th-, 6th-, 7th-grade
    girls), 18 minutes
Personal Products
Miltown, New Jersey

"World of a Girl"
Scott Paper Company, 1965,
Philadelphia, Pennsylvania